영어 리딩 학습의 최종 목표는 논픽션 독해력 향상에 있습니다.

학년이 올라갈수록 영어 시험 출제의 비중이 높아지는 논픽션. 우리는 논픽션 리딩을 통해 다양한 분야의 어휘와 지식을 습득하고 문제 해결 능력을 키울 수 있습니다. 또한 생활 속 실용문과 시험 상황의 복잡한 지문을 이해하고 분석하며, 나에게 필요한 정보를 추출하는 연습을 할 수 있습니다. 논픽션 독해력은 비판적 사고와 논리적 사고를 발전시키고, 영어로 표현된 아이디어를 깊이 있게 이해하고 효과적으로 소통하는 언어 능력을 갖출 수 있도록 도와줍니다.

미국교과서는 논픽션 리딩에 가장 적합한 학습 도구입니다.

미국교과서는 과학, 사회과학, 역사, 예술, 문학 등 다양한 주제의 폭넓은 지식과 이해를 제공하며, 사실을 그대로 받아들이는 능력뿐만 아니라 텍스트 너머의 맥락에 대한 비판적 사고와 분석 능력도 함께 배울 수 있도록 구성되어 있습니다. 미국 교과과정 주제의 리딩을 통해 학생들은 현실적인 주제를 탐구하고, 아카데믹한 어휘를 학습하면서 논리적 탐구의 방법을 함께 배울 수 있습니다. 미국교과서는 논픽션 독해력 향상을 위한 최고의 텍스트입니다.

탁월한 논픽션 독해력을 원한다면
미국교과서 READING 시리즈

1. 미국교과서의 핵심 주제들을 엄선하여 담은 지문을 읽으며 **독해력**이 향상되고 **배경지식**이 쌓입니다.

2. 가지고 있는 지식과 새로운 정보를 연결해 내 것으로 만드는 **통합사고력**을 기를 수 있습니다.

3. 꼼꼼히 읽고 완전히 소화할 수 있도록 하는 수준별 독해 훈련으로 **문제 해결력**이 향상됩니다.

4. 기초 문장 독해에서 추론까지, 학습자의 **수준별로 선택하여 학습**할 수 있도록 난이도를 설계하였습니다.

5. 스스로 계획하고 점검하며 실력을 쌓아가는 **자기주도력**이 형성됩니다.

Author Suejeong Shin

She has been an adjunct professor of English Education at Yonsei University since 2017. Her research centers around the implementation of cognitive psychology to foster literacy development among young English language learners in Korea. In addition to her role in the classroom, she demonstrates visionary leadership as the founder of We Read, a literacy company.

With an impressive collection of sixty children's picture book titles and over 200 literacy-focused textbooks, she is an accomplished author and an expert in her field. She actively engages in the development of an innovative literacy curation service, ensuring that children have positive reading experiences in English. Equipped with a Ph.D. in cognitive science from Yonsei University, Suejeong's transformative work can be further explored on her captivating website at www.drsue.co.kr.

미국교과서 READING **LEVEL 2** ❶
American Textbook Reading *Second Edition*

Second Published on August 14, 2023
Third Printed on November 15, 2024

First Published on November 27, 2015

Written by Suejeong Shin
Researcher Dain Song
Editorial Manager Namhui Kim, Seulgi Han
Design Kichun Jang, Hyeonsook Lee
Development Editor Mina Park
Proofreading Ryan P. Lagace, Benjamin Schultz
Typesetting Yeon Design
Illustrations Eunhyung Ryu, Hyoju Kim, Jongeun Yang
Recording Studio YR Media
Photo Credit shutterstock.com

Published and distributed by Gilbutschool
56, Worldcup-ro 10-gil, Mapo-gu, Seoul, Korea, 121-842
Tel 02-332-0931
Fax 02-322-0586
Homepage www.gilbutschool.co.kr
Publisher Jongwon Lee

ISBN   979-11-6406-541-7 (64740)
        979-11-6406-536-3 (set)
(Gilbutschool code : 30539)

미국교과서 리딩

READING

LEVEL 2 ①

길벗스쿨

★ 이 책의 특징 ★

LEVEL 2 논픽션 리딩 시작

1 **미국 교과과정 주제의 픽션(50%)과 논픽션(50%) 지문을 고루 읽으며 균형 있는 읽기 실력을 키웁니다.**

학생들의 인지 수준과 흥미를 반영한 다양한 토픽으로 하나의 주제 아래 Fiction과 Nonfiction 지문을 고루 읽을 수 있습니다. 이와 같은 반복적인 접근을 통하여 교과 주제에 더욱 익숙해지고 생각의 폭을 넓힐 수 있습니다.

2 **기초 논픽션 주제 어휘와 패턴 문형을 중심으로 다양한 형식의 글을 학습합니다.**

본격 논픽션 리딩 학습을 시작하기 전, 반복되는 패턴 문형 안에서 낯선 논픽션 어휘에 적응할 수 있도록 합니다. 또한 스토리 형식이나 설명문과 더불어 메뉴판, 편지글, 안내문 등 다양한 문형을 통하여 실용적인 텍스트를 이해하는 기초를 다집니다.

3 **간단한 문장 구조의 글을 읽고, 다양한 문제를 경험하며 독해의 기본기를 튼튼하게 합니다.**

지문을 읽고 핵심 주제, 세부 내용, 감정 표현, 문장 완성하기 등 다양한 문제를 통하여 읽은 내용을 파악합니다. 선택지에서 지문과 일치하는 부분을 찾아 단순히 답을 고르기 보다는 한번 더 생각하고 문제를 해결할 수 있도록 구성하여 독해의 기본기를 다집니다.

4 **도표를 활용한 전체 내용 통합 활동으로 기초 리딩 스킬을 연습합니다.**

도표 활동은 글의 구조를 확인하는 것과 동시에 어휘를 활용하는 능력에도 큰 도움이 됩니다. 길지 않은 지문이지만, 세부적인 내용을 확인한 이후 전체적으로 내용을 통합하고 정리하는 활동을 통하여 리딩 스킬을 익힐 수 있습니다.

Week 1

UNIT 01
Student Book ☐
Workbook ☐
DATE

UNIT 02
Student Book ☐
Workbook ☐

UNIT 03
Student Book ☐
Workbook ☐

UNIT 04
Student Book ☐
Workbook ☐

Week 2

UNIT 05
Student Book ☐
Workbook ☐
DATE

UNIT 06
Student Book ☐
Workbook ☐

UNIT 07
Student Book ☐
Workbook ☐

UNIT 08
Student Book ☐
Workbook ☐

Week 3

UNIT 09
Student Book ☐
Workbook ☐
DATE

UNIT 10
Student Book ☐
Workbook ☐

UNIT 11
Student Book ☐
Workbook ☐

UNIT 12
Student Book ☐
Workbook ☐

Week 4

UNIT 13
Student Book ☐
Workbook ☐
DATE

UNIT 14
Student Book ☐
Workbook ☐

UNIT 15
Student Book ☐
Workbook ☐

UNIT 16
Student Book ☐
Workbook ☐

Week 5

UNIT 17
Student Book ☐
Workbook ☐
DATE

UNIT 18
Student Book ☐
Workbook ☐

UNIT 19
Student Book ☐
Workbook ☐

UNIT 20
Student Book ☐
Workbook ☐

★ 이 책의 구성과 학습법 ★

Before Reading

배경지식을 묻는 질문에 답하고,
주제별 어휘를 익히며 글의 내용을 예측해 봅니다.

QR코드를 스캔하여
정확한 발음 확인하기

Talk About It

경험을 묻는 질문에 답하며
주제를 대략적으로 파악해
보고, 배경지식을 활성화
합니다.

Words to Know

단어를 듣고 따라 말하며
익히고, 그림을 통해 뜻을
유추합니다.

Reading

미국교과서 핵심 주제의 픽션, 논픽션 글을 읽으며
교과 지식과 독해력을 쌓습니다.

Reading Passage

제목과 그림을 통해 내용을
먼저 예측해 봅니다.
음원을 들으면서 글을 읽고,
중심 내용과 세부 내용을
파악합니다.

Key Expressions

글에 사용된 패턴 문형
대화를 듣고 따라 말하며
익힙니다.

After Reading

다양한 유형의 문제를 풀며 읽은 내용을 확인하고,
단어와 문장을 점검합니다.

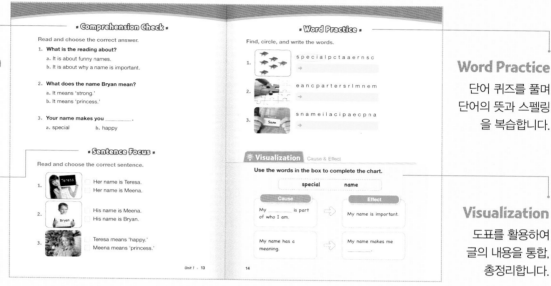

Comprehension Check

글의 주제와 세부
내용을 올바르게
이해했는지 확인합
니다.

Sentence Focus

그림에 알맞은 문장
을 고르며 패턴 문형
을 복습합니다.

Word Practice

단어 퀴즈를 풀며
단어의 뜻과 스펠링
을 복습합니다.

Visualization

도표를 활용하여
글의 내용을 통합,
총정리합니다.

Workbook

핵심 어휘와 주요 문장을
복습합니다.

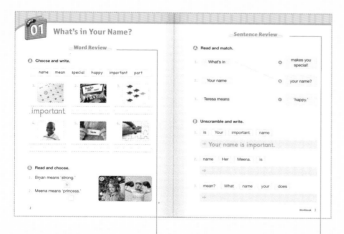

Word Review

이미지를 활용하여 단어의
의미를 복습합니다.

Sentence Review

문장 완성하기, 순서 배열하기
활동으로 패턴 문형과
어순을 복습합니다.

무료 온라인 학습 자료

길벗스쿨 e클래스

(eclass.gilbut.co.kr)에
접속하시면 〈미국교과서
READING〉시리즈에 대한
상세 정보 및 부가학습 자료를
무료로 이용하실 수 있습니다.

1. 음원 스트리밍 및 MP3 파일
2. 추가 워크시트 4종
   단어 테스트, 문장 따라 쓰기, 해석 테스트,
   리딩 지문 테스트
3. 복습용 온라인 퀴즈

★ 목차 ★

What's in Your Name?

• Words to Know •

Listen and repeat. 🎧

name

important

part

mean

happy

strong

princess

special

What's in Your Name? 🎧

What's in your name?
Your name is important.
It is part of who you are.
What does your name mean?

Her name is Teresa.
Teresa means 'happy.'

His name is Bryan.
Bryan means 'strong.'

Her name is Meena.
Meena means 'princess.'

Your name makes you special!

▲ Teresa means
'happy' in Chinese.

▲ Bryan means
'strong' in English.

▲ Meena means
'princess' in Hindi.

Hello!
My name is
_____.

💬 **Key Expressions**
A: What does your name mean?
B: My name means 'happy.'

▪ Comprehension Check ▪

Read and choose the correct answer.

1. **What is the reading about?**

   a. It is about funny names.

   b. It is about why a name is important.

2. **What does the name Bryan mean?**

   a. It means 'strong.'

   b. It means 'princess.'

3. **Your name makes you _____ .**

   a. special   **b.** happy

▪ Sentence Focus ▪

Read and choose the correct sentence.

1.
   ☐ Her name is Teresa.
   ☐ Her name is Meena.

2.
   ☐ His name is Meena.
   ☐ His name is Bryan.

3.
   ☐ Teresa means 'happy.'
   ☐ Meena means 'princess.'

▪ Word Practice ▪

Find, circle, and write the words.

1.

   (s p e c i a l)p c t a a e r n s c

   ➜

2.

   e a n c p a r t e r s r l m n e m

   ➜

3.

   s n a m e i l a c i p a e c p n a

   ➜

☼ Visualization   Cause & Effect

Use the words in the box to complete the chart.

| special | name |

Cause		**Effect**
My _____ is part of who I am.	⇨	My name is important.
My name has a meaning.	⇨	My name makes me _____.

The Alphabet

B C D E F G H I J
a K L M N O Q P r S
t u w
X Y Z

Talk About It 🎧

1 What do you know about the alphabet?
2 Can you sing 'The Alphabet Song?'

• Words to Know •

Listen and repeat. 🎧

alphabet

start

end

between

20

twenty

26

twenty-six

letter

guess

The Alphabet 🎧

The alphabet starts with ABC.

It always ends with XYZ.

And in between are twenty other letters.

That makes twenty-six letters all together.

There are four letters in my name.

My name starts with the letter D.

My name ends with the letter N.

Can you guess my name?

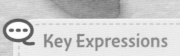

💬 **Key Expressions**

A: What does your name start with?

B: My name starts with R.

Comprehension Check

Read and choose the correct answer.

1. What is the reading about?

a. It is about numbers.

b. It is about the alphabet.

2. How many letters are there in the alphabet?

a. There are twenty letters.

b. There are twenty-six letters.

3. My name is _____.

a. Dan   b. Dain

Sentence Focus

Read and choose the correct sentence.

1.
   ☐ The alphabet starts with ABC.
   ☐ The alphabet starts with XYZ.

2.
   ☐ My name ends with the letter D.
   ☐ My name ends with the letter N.

3.
   ☐ There are four letters in my name.
   ☐ There are twenty-six letters in my name.

Word Practice

Find, circle, and write the words.

1. e e e s u l e g n e t e (g u e s s)

   →

2. n e e b w e b e t w e e n e e e g

   →

3. r t n e t e t e l e t t e r n n s

   →

Visualization · Main Idea & Details

Use the words in the box to complete the chart.

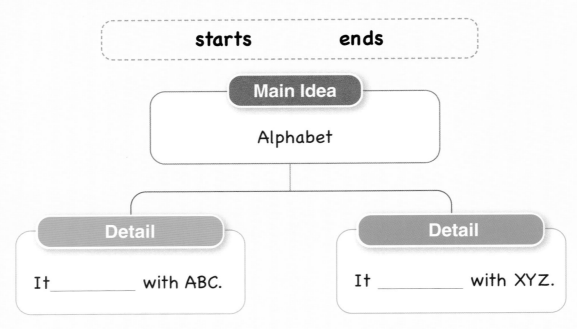

starts   ends

Main Idea

Alphabet

Detail

It _____ with ABC.

Detail

It _____ with XYZ.

Happy Birthday!

Talk About It 🎧

1 When is your birthday?
2 What do you do on your birthday?

▪ Words to Know ▪

Listen and repeat. 🎧

birthday

popsicle

doughnut

stomachache

sick

party hat

party horn

friend

Happy Birthday!

Yesterday, I went to a party.

I had a popsicle.

I had a doughnut.

I had cake.

I had a stomachache!

Today, I am sick in bed.

I have a party hat.

I have a party horn.

I have no friends with me.

Happy birthday to me!

No
Visitors
Allowed

Get
well
Soon!

Get well
Soon!

Key Expressions
- I had a popsicle.
- I have a party hat.

20

▪ Comprehension Check ▪

Read and choose the correct answer.

1. What special day is today?

   a. Today is my birthday.

   b. Today is Christmas.

2. How am I today?

   a. I am happy at home.

   b. I am sick in bed.

3. I have no _____ with me today.

   a. friends   **b.** party hats

▪ Sentence Focus ▪

Read and choose the correct sentence.

1.
☐ I had a doughnut.
☐ I had cake.

2.
☐ I had a popsicle.
☐ I had a stomachache.

3.
☐ I have a party hat.
☐ I have a party horn.

▪ Word Practice ▪

Find, circle, and write the words.

1.    y i t y t o o s s i c k p h e r p

2.    h p e h y a p o p s i c l e c i i

3.   t p a r t y h a t p p s s s i i s

⚙ Visualization   Cause & Effect

Use the words in the box to complete the chart.

> birthday   stomachache

Why?		What Happened?
I had a popsicle. I had a doughnut. I had cake.		I had a _____.
Today is my _____.		I have a party hat and a party horn.

Birthday Goodies

Talk About It 🎧

1 What birthday goodies do you know?
2 Do you like popsicles?

• Words to Know •

Listen and repeat. 🎧

gummy bear

soda

mold

fill

pour

poke

freeze

enjoy

Birthday Goodies 🎧

Let's Make Gummy Bear Popsicles for Birthday!

What you need:
gummy bears, mold, soda

What you do:
1. Fill molds with gummy bears.
2. Pour soda in each mold.
3. Poke a popsicle stick in the center of each mold.
4. Freeze for at least 5 hours.
5. Enjoy your popsicles!

💬 Key Expressions
A: Pour soda in each mold.
B: OK.

▪ Comprehension Check ▪

Read and choose the correct answer.

1. What is the reading about?

    a. It is about how to eat popsicles.

    b. It is about how to make popsicles.

2. What do you need to make popsicles?

    a. I need bears.

    b. I need molds.

3. You need to wait at least _____ hours.

    a. five   **b.** nine

▪ Sentence Focus ▪

Read and choose the correct sentence.

1.
   ☐ Fill molds with gummy bears.
   ☐ Fill molds with soda.

2.
   ☐ Poke soda in each mold.
   ☐ Pour soda in each mold.

3.
   ☐ Find a popsicle stick in the center of each mold.
   ☐ Poke a popsicle stick in the center of each mold.

▪ Word Practice ▪

Find, circle, and write the words.

1. j j e f s s s e n e e n j o y d a

    ➡

2. e o a f r e e z e y a s n y y z e

    ➡

3. s o s o d a f e f o e n d o r a j

    ➡

🔆 Visualization   Sequence

Use the words in the box to complete the chart. Then number 1-4 to show the correct order.

Fill   Poke

3			
_____ a popsicle stick in each mold.	Pour soda in each mold.	_____ molds with gummy bears.	Freeze for at least 5 hours.

26

Where Is It?

Talk About It

1 How many teeth do you have?
2 Do you have any loose teeth?

· Words to Know ·

Listen and repeat.

lost tooth

pillow

blanket

dresser

curtain

picture

clock

drawer

Where Is It?

I've come to get Leo's first lost tooth.
I have to look under the pillow.
Oh, oh! Where is Leo's lost tooth?

Is it under his blanket?
Is it on his dresser?
Is it in his drawer?
Is it between his picture and
clock?
Is it behind his curtain?

Where is his lost tooth?
Oh, it was in his hand!

Key Expressions
A: Where is Leo's lost tooth?
B: It is in his hand.

■ Comprehension Check ■

Read and choose the correct answer.

1. Who am I?

    a. I am Leo.

    b. I am the tooth fairy.

2. Where was Leo's lost tooth?

    a. It was in his drawer.

    b. It was in his hand.

3. I've come to get Leo's _____ lost tooth.

    a. first   **b.** second

■ Sentence Focus ■

Read and choose the correct sentence.

1.
  ☐ I have to look under the bed.
  ☐ I have to look under the blanket.

2.
  ☐ Is it on his dresser?
  ☐ Is it behind his curtain?

3.
  ☐ Where is his lost tooth?
  ☐ Where is his lost clock?

■ Word Practice ■

Find, circle, and write the words.

1.  e c o i c e c l o c k t u c p t u

   →

2.  u c c k c t u l c c p i c t u r e

   →

3.  r t c u r t a i n a e k r u t k l

   →

☼ **Visualization** Problem & Solution

Use the words in the box to complete the chart.

dresser   lost tooth

Problem	Solution
Where is Leo's _____?	I have to look under the pillow.
	I have to look on the _____.

Your Eyes Play Tricks

1. What do you see in the picture?
2. Do you think the circles are moving?

Words to Know

Listen and repeat. 🎧

see

number

man

woman

vase

pyramid

queen

trick

Your Eyes Play Tricks

Look closely at these pictures.
What do you see?

Sometimes, you see letters.
But sometimes, you see numbers.

Sometimes, you see a man and a woman.
But sometimes, you see a vase.

Sometimes, you see a man between the pyramids.
But sometimes, you see a queen of Egypt.

What you think you see is often not the truth.
Your eyes play tricks!

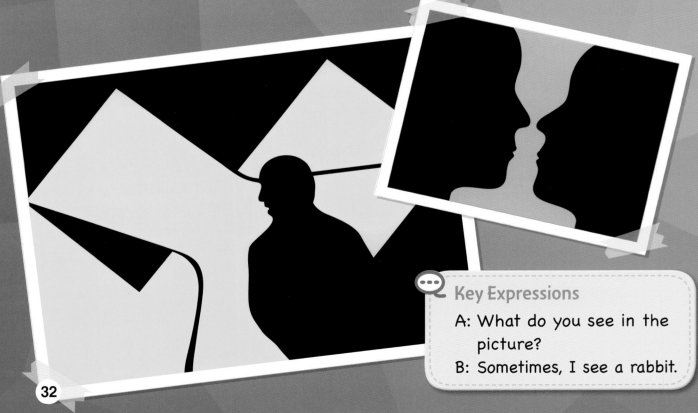

Key Expressions

A: What do you see in the picture?
B: Sometimes, I see a rabbit.

▪ Comprehension Check ▪

Read and choose the correct answer.

1. **What is the reading about?**

   a. It's about how to think.

   b. It's about what you see.

2. **Why do you sometimes not see the whole picture?**

   a. Because my eyes play tricks.

   b. Because I have bad eyesight.

3. **What you think you see is often not the _____.**

   a. picture   **b.** truth

▪ Sentence Focus ▪

Read and choose the correct sentence.

1.
☐ Sometimes, you see a man.
☐ Sometimes, you see a queen.

2.
☐ Look closely at these pyramids.
☐ Look closely at these numbers.

3.
☐ Your eyes play tricks!
☐ Your friends play tricks!

■ Word Practice ■

Find, circle, and write the words.

1.
n m a n n m i a o r n k n a w k

→

2.
i m t m c k i i n a t w o m a n i

→

3.
a n o o k w a o c w t r i c k a c

→

☼ Visualization   Cause & Effect

Use the words in the box to complete the chart.

letters   tricks

Why?		What Happened?
		Sometimes, I see _____.
Your eyes play _____. 		But sometimes, I see numbers.

I Am Late!

Talk About It 🎧

1. What time do you get up?
2. What time does your school start?

▪ Words to Know ▪

Listen and repeat. 🎧

late

grab

push

hurry

downstairs

upstairs

put

Sunday

I Am Late! 🎧

Oh, no!
I got up late for school!
I grab my bag.
I push my bedroom door open.
I hurry downstairs.

Oh, no!
I forgot my books!
I go back upstairs.
I quickly put my books in
my bag.
I go back downstairs.

"It's Sunday, Ron!" says Mom.

I forgot!
It's Sunday today!

💬 **Key Expressions**
A: I got up late for school.
B: It's Sunday today.

▪ Comprehension Check ▪

Read and choose the correct answer.

1. **Why do I hurry?**

   a. Because I got up late for school.

   b. Because I forgot my books.

2. **What day is today?**

   a. Today is Sunday.

   b. Today is a school day.

3. **I go back upstairs and _____ my books in my bag.**

   a. push   b. put

▪ Sentence Focus ▪

Read and choose the correct sentence.

1.
   ☐ I push the door.
   ☐ I push the bag.

2.
   ☐ I go back upstairs.
   ☐ I go back downstairs.

3.
   ☐ I put my books in my bag.
   ☐ I put my shoes in my bag.

▪ Word Practice ▪

Find, circle, and write the words.

1.

   h l l l a t e (t r r) y t p a u h l

   →

2.

   r y a h u r r y r l u p u t p y l

   →

3.

   a y t p a a a p r y a t p u t e h

   →

🔆 Visualization Setting

Use the words in the box to complete the chart.

> push   Sunday

What?		**What?**
I grab my bag.	**When?**	I hurry downstairs.
I _____ my bedroom door open.	It's _____ today.	I go back upstairs.
What?		**What?**

What's for Breakfast?

Talk About It 🎧

1 Do you eat breakfast every morning?
2 What do you like for breakfast?

▪ Words to Know ▪

Listen and repeat. 🎧

eat

breakfast

fruit

noodle

pancake

corn flakes

porridge

bread

What's for Breakfast? 🎧

Kids around the world eat breakfast.

Some kids eat fruit for breakfast.
Some kids eat noodles for breakfast.
Some kids eat pancakes for breakfast.
Some kids eat corn flakes for breakfast.
Some kids eat porridge for breakfast.
Some kids eat bread for breakfast.

Every kid eats breakfast!

▼ Egypt Pita Bread

▼ Brazil Fruit

▼ United States Pancakes

▼ Vietnam Noodles

▼ Russia Porridge

▲ Australia Corn Flakes

💬 **Key Expressions**

A: What do kids eat for breakfast?
B: Some kids eat fruit.

Comprehension Check

Read and choose the correct answer.

1. **What is the reading about?**

    a. It's about kids.

    b. It's about breakfast.

2. **What do kids eat for breakfast?**

    a. Some kids eat snowflakes for breakfast.

    b. Some kids eat bread for breakfast.

3. **In the picture, a little girl eats _____ for breakfast.**

    a. noodles   **b.** bread

Sentence Focus

Read and choose the correct sentence.

1.
   ☐ Some kids eat fruit for breakfast.
   ☐ Some kids eat noodles for breakfast.

2. ☐ Every kid eats bread.
   ☐ Every kid eats porridge.

3. ☐ Some kids eat pancakes.
   ☐ Some kids eat corn flakes.

▪ Word Practice ▪

Find, circle, and write the words.

1.    f r i u r a r e i i e a t f a t d

   →

2.    t b r e a d e e i e r a e a i e a

   →

3.    i r i b e a a t b r f r u i t e e

   →

☀ Visualization   Main Idea & Details

Use the words in the box to complete the chart.

Breakfast   noodles

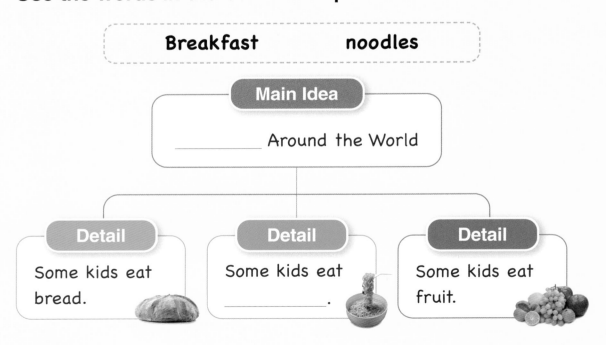

Main Idea

_____ Around the World

Detail

Some kids eat bread.

Detail

Some kids eat _____ .

Detail

Some kids eat fruit.

Who Will Help Me?

Talk About It

1 What are the children in the photo doing?
2 Why is it a good idea to help others?

• Words to Know •

Listen and repeat.

help

plant

pick

make

giraffe

snore

corn

popcorn

Who Will Help Me? 🎧

"Who will help me plant corn?"
asked Giraffe.
"We will," said Cat and Dog.

"Who will help me pick the corn?" asked Giraffe.
"We will," said Cat and Dog.

"Who will help me make popcorn?" asked Giraffe.
"We will," said Cat and Dog.

"Who will help me eat the popcorn?" asked Giraffe.
"Not we," said Cat and Dog.

"Oh, no!" said Giraffe.
"Zzzzz…" snored Cat and Dog.

💬 **Key Expressions**
A: Who will help me make popcorn?
B: I will.

44

Comprehension Check

Read and choose the correct answer.

1. Who asked help?

   a. Cat and Dog

   b. Giraffe

2. What did Cat, Dog, and Giraffe do?

   a. They picked the corn.

   b. They snored.

3. Cat and Dog helped Giraffe make _____.

   a. corn   **b.** popcorn

Sentence Focus

Read and choose the correct sentence.

1.
   ☐ Who will help me pick the corn?
   ☐ Who will help me pick the popcorn?

2.
   ☐ Who will help me eat the corn?
   ☐ Who will help me eat the popcorn?

3.
   ☐ Cat and Dog snored.
   ☐ Dog and Giraffe snored.

Word Practice

Find, circle, and write the words.

1.  n p p ⟨c o r n⟩ p i r p e r c o p o

   →

2. n l c k o e k r r e c h e l p n e

   →

3. n p i c k i i p l h l o k p h k c

   →

Visualization Sequence

Use the words in the box to complete the chart. Then number 1-4 to show the correct order.

make   plant

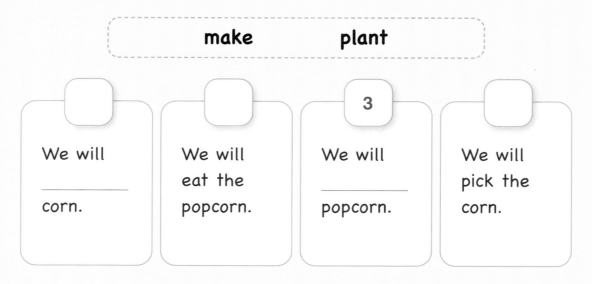

		3	
We will _____ corn.	We will eat the popcorn.	We will _____ popcorn.	We will pick the corn.

Animals' Sleep

Talk About It

1 When do animals sleep?
2 How much do animals sleep?

· Words to Know ·

Listen and repeat.

| animal | sleep | day | night |

| a lot | little | hour | human |

Animals' Sleep 🎧

Some animals sleep during the day.
Some animals sleep during the night.

Some animals sleep a lot.
Some animals sleep very little.

How much do animals sleep?

Animals	Average Total Sleep Time / Day
Bat	19.9 hours
Sloth	14.4 hours
Cat	12.1 hours
Dog	10.6 hours
Human	8.6 hours
Giraffe	1.9 hours

▲ This animal sleeps 14.4 hours a day.

▲ I sleep 8 hours a day.

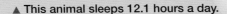

▲ This animal sleeps 12.1 hours a day.

💬 Key Expressions

A: How much do cats sleep?
B: They sleep 12.1 hours a day.

48

Comprehension Check

Read and choose the correct answer.

1. **What is the reading about?**

   a. It's about animals' sleep.

   b. It's about animal names.

2. **Which animal sleeps more?**

   a. a cat

   b. a giraffe

3. **Humans sleep about _____ hours a day.**

   a. 10   **b.** 8

Sentence Focus

Read and choose the correct sentence.

1.
   - ☐ A giraffe sleeps a lot.
   - ☐ A giraffe sleeps very little.

2.
   - ☐ A bat sleeps during the day.
   - ☐ A bat sleeps during the night.

3.
   - ☐ This animal sleeps 14.4 hours a day.
   - ☐ This animal sleeps 10.6 hours a day.

■ Word Practice ■

Find, circle, and write the words.

1.    s d n e y d a a e d a d d a y y e
   →

2.    p e a l s l e e p d e a n n y p l
   →

3.   e p y d a a n i m a l i i l e y s
   →

☼ Visualization   Main Idea & Details

Use the words in the box to complete the chart.

hours   Sleep

Main Idea

Animals' _____

Detail	Detail	Detail
Some animals sleep during the day.	Some animals sleep a lot.	Some animals sleep 1.9 _____ a day.

Weather

UNIT **11** Science

▪ Words to Know ▪

Listen and repeat.

wet

dry

hot

cold

wind

cloudy

rain

change

Weather

Look out the window.

Is it wet or dry?
Are there clouds?
Can you see the sun?
Is there wind?
How hot or cold is it?

It was cloudy in the morning.
Then, it rained.
Now, we have a strong wind.

Whether we like it or not,
the weather changes all the time.

▪ Comprehension Check ▪

Read and choose the correct answer.

1. What is the reading about?

   a. It's about windows.

   b. It's about the weather.

2. How is the weather now?

   a. It is rainy.

   b. It is windy.

3. The weather _____ all the time.

   a. changes   **b.** rains

▪ Sentence Focus ▪

Read and choose the correct sentence.

1.
☐ It is wet today.
☐ It is dry today.

2.
☐ It was cold in the morning.
☐ It was hot in the morning.

3.
☐ We have a heavy rain.
☐ We have a strong wind.

▪ Word Practice ▪

Find, circle, and write the words.

1.

   r w o c d c d r y l d d w d w w r

   →

2.

   n y o l d d d r o d y c o l d d l

   →

3.

   i d i d r c y w i n d a d d w n l

   →

⚙ Visualization Summarize

Use the words in the box to complete the chart.

> changes   cloudy

- It was _____ in the morning.
- Then, it rained.
- Now, we have a strong wind.

Summary

The weather _____ all the time.

Let's Play with Tangrams

Talk About It

1 Do you like rainy days?

2 What do you like to do on a rainy day?

Words to Know

Listen and repeat.

tangram

puzzle

triangle

square

rectangle

people

thing

quickly

Let's Play with Tangrams

It is raining outside.
It is a perfect day to play with a tangram.
A tangram is a Chinese puzzle.

You can make a large square, rectangle, or triangle.
You can make shapes of animals.
You can make shapes of people.
You can make shapes of things.

Do you want to play, too?
See how quickly you can make each puzzle.
Have fun!

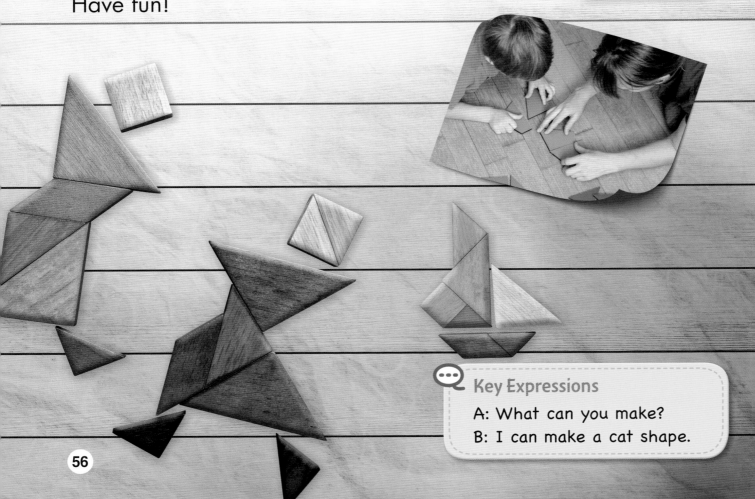

Key Expressions

A: What can you make?
B: I can make a cat shape.

56

Comprehension Check

Read and choose the correct answer.

1. What is the reading about?

   a. It's about what a tangram is.

   b. It's about a perfect day.

2. What can you do with a tangram?

   a. I can meet people.

   b. I can make shapes of animals.

3. In the picture, _____ pieces are used to make a cat shape.

   a. seven   b. eight

Sentence Focus

Read and choose the correct sentence.

1.

   ☐ It is a perfect day to play outside.
   ☐ It is a perfect day to play with a puzzle.

2.

   ☐ You can make shapes of animals.
   ☐ You can make shapes of people.

3.
   ☐ You can make a large square.
   ☐ You can make a large triangle.

▪ Word Practice ▪

Find, circle, and write the words.

1.

p l e e u g p i z p p e (t h i n g)

→ _____

2.

t p e e i p e o p l e e n p n n l

→ _____

3.

e z p t i e p e p u z z l e p t p

→ _____

🔆 Visualization   Main Idea & Details

Use the words in the box to complete the chart.

Chinese   quickly   things

Main Idea

Tangram

Detail

It's a _____ puzzle.

Detail

You can make shapes of animals, people, and _____ .

Detail

It's fun to make each puzzle _____ .

What a Team!

Talk About It 🎧

1 Have you seen dogs helping people?
2 How do dogs help people?

▪ Words to Know ▪

Listen and repeat. 🎧

bark

hole

search

dig

snow

trapped

leap

wag

What a Team! 🎧

"Woof, woof!"
Kevin barks at a hole.

I run to Kevin.
I give Kevin the order "Search!"

Kevin quickly digs the hole bigger.
And I pull out the man trapped in snow.

"Good boy, Kevin, good boy!" I pet Kevin.
Kevin leaps and wags his tail.

Kevin and I,
we make a good team!

Key Expressions
A: How do some dogs help people?
B: Some dogs rescue people.

60

Comprehension Check

Read and choose the correct answer.

1. **Why does Kevin bark?**

   a. Because Kevin is trapped in snow.

   b. Because Kevin finds a man trapped in snow.

2. **What does Kevin do?**

   a. Kevin digs the hole bigger.

   b. Kevin pulls out the man.

3. **Kevin is a rescue _____ .**

   a. boy   b. dog

Sentence Focus

Read and choose the correct sentence.

1.
   - ☐ Kevin barks at a hole.
   - ☐ Kevin digs a hole bigger.

2.
   - ☐ I give Kevin the order.
   - ☐ I pull out the man trapped in snow.

3.
   - ☐ Kevin leaps over his trail.
   - ☐ Kevin wags his tail.

Word Practice

Find, circle, and write the words.

1. d e e o p l r r c t a h o l e a e

   →

2. c h l h t o p o s e a r c h l o r

   →

3. e o a c d p e a t r a p p e d o d

   →

Visualization Story Elements

Use the words in the box to complete the chart.

order   snow

Who?	What?	Why?
Kevin and I	1. Kevin barks at a hole. 2. I give Kevin the _____ "Search!" 3. Kevin quickly digs the hole bigger.	Kevin and I have to rescue the man trapped in _____.

62

Camouflage

Talk About It 🎧

1 What do you see in the picture?
2 What will the mouse do?

• Words to Know •

Listen and repeat. 🎧

hide

hard

caterpillar

branch

jaguar

nest

pattern

wild

Camouflage 🎧

How do animals hide in the wild?

This caterpillar is hard to see on a branch.
This jaguar is hard to see in the trees.
This fish is hard to see in the sand.

These eggs are hard to see in the nest.
These birds are hard to see in the grass.
These snakes are hard to see in the tree.

Animals use colors or patterns
to hide in the wild.

💬 **Key Expressions**

A: How do some animals hide?
B: They use colors to hide.

Comprehension Check

Read and choose the correct answer.

1. What is the reading about?

   a. It's about how animals hide.

   b. It's about how animals see.

2. Why are jaguars hard to see in the trees?

   a. Because jaguars use patterns to hide.

   b. Because jaguars use eyes to hide.

3. Animals use colors or patterns to _____ in the wild.

   a. play   b. hide

Sentence Focus

Read and choose the correct sentence.

1.
   ☐ This fish is hard to see in the sand.
   ☐ This egg is hard to see in the sand.

2.
   ☐ This bird is hard to see in the trees.
   ☐ This bird is hard to see in the grass.

3.
   ☐ This snake uses colors to hide in the wild.
   ☐ This snake uses patterns to hide in the wild.

▪ Word Practice ▪

Find, circle, and write the words.

1.  (b r a n c h) r n n r r h r e c h a d

→

2.  d h n n n b a i d d b h h i d e h

→

3. c b i i e e c w i l d e e a w d i

→

⚙ Visualization   Main Idea & Details

Use the words in the box to complete the chart.

hide   patterns

Main Idea

Animals _____
from other animals
in the wild.

Details

· Some animals use colors to hide.

· Some animals use _____ to hide.

UNIT 15

Social Studies

Winter Carnival

Talk About It 🎧

1 Have you ever received or sent postcards?
2 When do people send postcards?

▪ Words to Know ▪

Listen and repeat. 🎧

weather

Canada

winter

carnival

dogsled racing

snow tubing

ice hotel

visit

Winter Carnival

Dear Grandma,

I'm writing to you from Québec, Canada.

The weather is cold and snowy.

I visited the Québec Winter Carnival.

I enjoyed dogsled racing.

I enjoyed snow tubing.

I enjoyed staying in an ice hotel.

I like it here in Québec.

You should visit here!

I hope we can come here together next time!

Love from Sarah

💬 **Key Expressions**

A: What did you do in Québec?
B: I enjoyed dogsled racing.

▪ Comprehension Check ▪

Read and choose the correct answer.

1. Where did Sarah visit?

  a. She visited the Québec Winter Carnival.

  b. She visited her Grandma's house in Québec.

2. What did Sarah enjoy at the winter carnival?

  a. She enjoyed snow tubing.

  b. She enjoyed skating.

3. Sarah is writing a postcard to her _____ .

  a. friend   **b.** grandma

▪ Sentence Focus ▪

Read and choose the correct sentence.

1.
☐ I visited Canada.
☐ I visited Korea.

2.
☐ I enjoyed dogsled racing.
☐ I enjoyed snow tubing.

3.
☐ I stayed in an ice hotel.
☐ I stayed in a tent.

■ Word Practice ■

Find, circle, and write the words.

1.
   n w (w i n t e r) i a i i c l i i r
   →

2.
   a d c a r n i v a l c c s i n r c
   →

3.
   r e n i i s l a n r n v i s i t e
   →

⚙ Visualization   Main Idea & Details

Use the word box to complete the chart.

> ice hotel   Winter

Main Idea

The Québec _____ Carnival

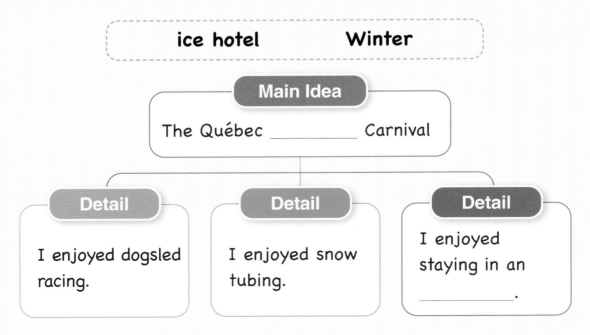

Detail

I enjoyed dogsled racing.

Detail

I enjoyed snow tubing.

Detail

I enjoyed staying in an _____.

70

What's for Lunch?

Talk About It 🎧

1 What do you want for your lunch today?
2 What do children eat around the world?

▪ Words to Know ▪

Listen and repeat. 🎧

local

add

crab

green salad

grilled

drink

bottled water

take-out

What's for Lunch? 🎧

ALASKA FISH HOUSE
KETCHIKAN

FISH

	2 pieces	3 pieces
Sea Cod	$10.00	$12.00
Local Salmon	$11.00	$13.00
Local Halibut	$16.00	$18.00

CRAB

½ lb. Spider	$14.00
1 lb. Spider	$27.00
½ lb. King	$22.00
1 lb. King	$43.00

SALAD

Green Salad	$5.00
Add Grilled Salmon	$6.00
Add Grilled Halibut	$7.00

DRINKS

Soda (small)	$1.00
(large)	$2.00
Orange Juice	$3.00
Bottled Water	$2.00

Happy Hour!
Monday-Friday 3PM-6PM
"TAKE-OUT AVAILABLE"

 Key Expressions

A: What do you want for lunch?
B: I want the local salmon, please.

72

Comprehension Check

Read and choose the correct answer.

1. **What is the reading?**

   a. It's a coupon.

   b. It's a menu.

2. **How much do 2 pieces of sea cod cost?**

   a. $10.00

   b. $11.00

3. **I need _____ to have a green salad.**

   a. $5.00   b. $9.00

Sentence Focus

Read and choose the correct sentence.

1. FISH

	2 pieces	3 pieces
Sea Cod	$10.00	$12.00
Local Salmon	$11.00	$13.00
Local Halibut	$16.00	$18.00

   ☐ I want the local halibut.

   ☐ I want the king crab.

2. CRAB

½ lb. Spider	$14.00
1 lb. Spider	$27.00
½ lb. King	$22.00
1 lb. King	$43.00

   ☐ I have $25. I can eat 1 lb. of spider crab.

   ☐ I have $25. I can eat ½ lb. of king crab.

3. DRINKS

Soda (small)	$1.00
(large)	$2.00
Orange Juice	$3.00
Bottled Water	$2.00

   ☐ I need $2 to drink a small soda.

   ☐ I need $2 to drink a large soda.

Word Practice

Find, circle, and write the words.

1. g d e r b r a l a d d d a d g a a

   →

2. g d r g c r a b l c b g a d a g c

   →

3. g r i l l e d i c e l g l r a d i

   →

☼ Visualization   Categorize

Use the words in the box to complete the chart.

Drinks   Fish

_____ and Crab	Salad	_____
· sea cod	· green salad	· small soda
· salmon	· grilled salmon salad	· large soda
· halibut	· grilled halibut salad	· orange juice
· spider crab		· bottled water
· king crab		

Will It Sink or Float?

Talk About It 🎧

1 What will happen if you put an apple in water?

2 Will an apple float or sink?

▪ Words to Know ▪

Listen and repeat. 🎧

splash

bath

bubble

wonder

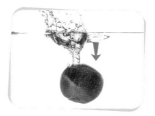

sink

float

tub

soap

Will It Sink or Float? 🎧

Andy loves to splash in the bath.

This is Little Rubber Duck.
He is Andy's bath time friend.
He can quack.
He can make some bubbles.
Andy wonders, 'Will he sink or will he float?'
Andy drops Little Rubber Duck into the tub.
He floats!
Andy finds soap, a toothbrush, a comb,
and a sponge.
One at a time, Andy puts them in the tub.
Will they sink or will they float?

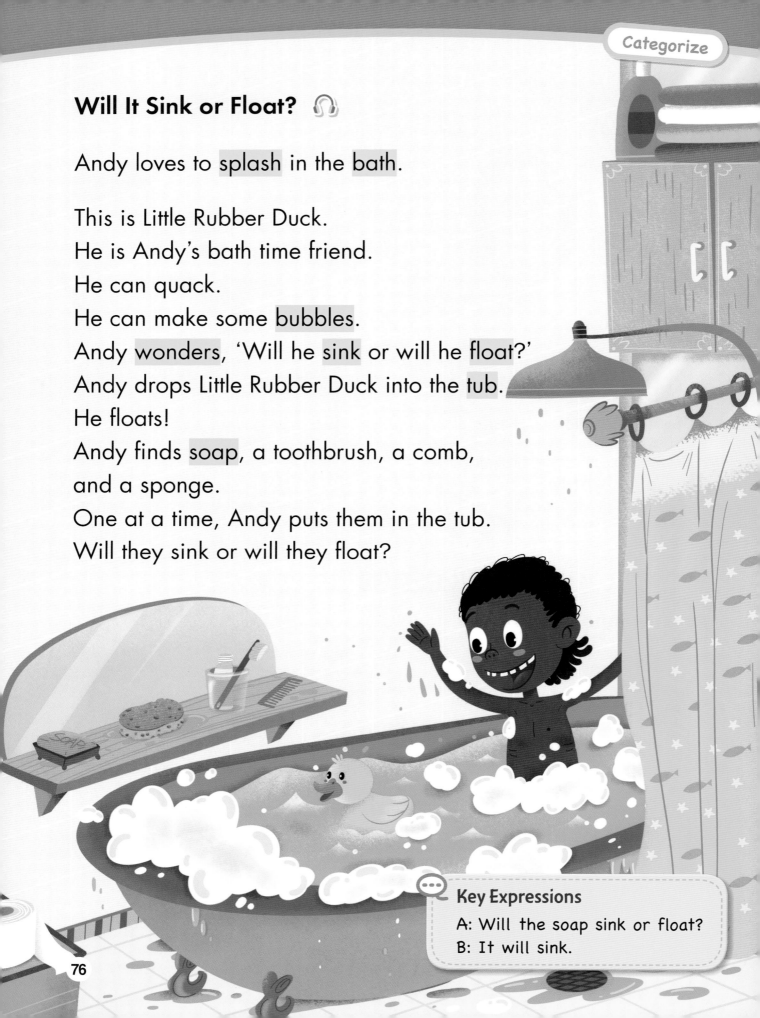

Key Expressions
A: Will the soap sink or float?
B: It will sink.

Comprehension Check

Read and choose the correct answer.

1. Where is Andy?

   a. Andy is in the bedroom.

   b. Andy is in the bathroom.

2. What does Andy do?

   a. Andy makes some bubbles.

   b. Andy splashes in the bath.

3. Little Rubber Duck _____ on the water.

   a. floats   b. sinks

Sentence Focus

Read and choose the correct sentence.

1.
   ☐ He can make some bubbles.
   ☐ He can quack.

2.
   ☐ He drops a toothbrush into the tub.
   ☐ He drops a sponge into the tub.

3.
   ☐ He loves to make bubbles.
   ☐ He loves to splash in the bath.

▪ Word Practice ▪

Find, circle, and write the words.

1.

   w w e k b h h b o a b k (b a t h) w

   → _____

2.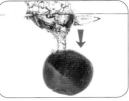

   e b b r d t w o n d e r t b w d e

   → _____

3.

   k n d n i s e s k a d e o s i n k

   → _____

⚙ Visualization   Categorize

Use the words in the box to complete the chart.

> sponge   Sink

Float	
• Little Rubber Duck	• a comb
• a _____	• soap
• a toothbrush	

Discover Matter

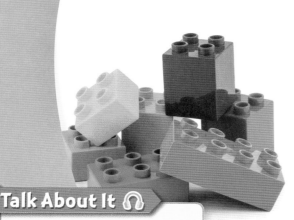

Talk About It 🎧

1 What can change shape?
2 What can change size?

▪ Words to Know ▪

Listen and repeat. 🎧

look

desk

solid

liquid

gas

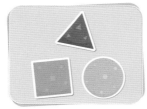

shape

size

matter

Discover Matter 🎧

Look all around.
Most of what you see is matter.

A desk is matter.
A desk is a solid.
A solid has a shape.

Milk is matter.
Milk is a liquid.
A liquid can change shape.

Air in a ball is matter.
Air in the ball is a gas.
A gas can change shape and size.

Solids, liquids, and gases are matter.
Solids, liquids, and gases are all around you.

💬 **Key Expressions**

A: What can change shape?
B: A liquid and a gas can change shape.

■ Comprehension Check ■

Read and choose the correct answer.

1. What is the reading about?

    a. It's about matter.

    b. It's about size.

2. Where can you see matter?

    a. I can see matter all around.

    b. I can see matter only in a ball.

3. A _____ can change shape and size.

    a. gas   **b.** solid

■ Sentence Focus ■

Read and choose the correct sentence.

1.
   ☐ A desk is solid.
   ☐ A desk is gas.

2.
   ☐ Air in a ball is a liquid.
   ☐ Air in a ball is a gas.

3.
   ☐ Liquid can change shape.
   ☐ Solid can change shape.

Find, circle, and write the words.

1.

l a l g s l o o k d s a l a s o k

→

2. d l s o l i d o i s s o o g d i s

→

3. s o i s k s k g a s o o i l g o s

→

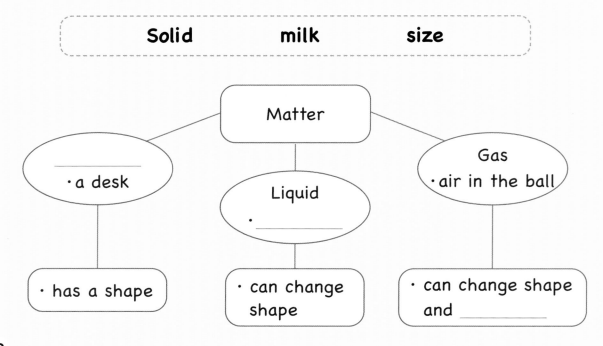

🔆 Visualization Categorize

Use the words in the box to complete the chart.

Solid   milk   size

Matter

(_____)
·a desk

Liquid
· _____

Gas
·air in the ball

· has a shape

· can change shape

· can change shape and _____

The Story of Ayo

Talk About It 🎧

1 What are children in the picture doing?
2 Do you think it is safe to drink the water?

▪ Words to Know ▪

Listen and repeat. 🎧

dirty

clean

skin

stomach

head

hurt

wake

get

The Story of Ayo 🎧

Ayo lives in Zambia.
She lives with her sister, Amara.
The water is very dirty in Zambia.
It makes Ayo's skin hurt.
It makes Ayo's stomach hurt.
It makes Ayo's head hurt.
Every morning Amara wakes up before the sun.
She walks two miles to get water for Ayo.
She walks three times a day to get water for Ayo.
Ayo feels sorry for Amara.
Ayo wishes they could have clean
water in Zambia.

💬 **Key Expressions**

A: What will happen if you
   drink dirty water?
B: It will make my skin hurt.

▪ Comprehension Check ▪

Read and choose the correct answer.

1. Who is the story about?

   a. It's about Zambia.

   b. It's about Ayo.

2. What's the problem in Zambia?

   a. The air is very dirty.

   b. The water is very dirty.

3. Ayo wishes for _____ water in Zambia.

   a. clean   **b.** dirty

▪ Sentence Focus ▪

Read and choose the correct sentence.

1.
   ☐ She lives with her sister.
   ☐ She lives with her mom.

2.
   ☐ She wakes up before Ayo.
   ☐ She wakes up before the sun.

3.
   ☐ She walks two miles to get water.
   ☐ She walks two miles to see her sister.

▪ Word Practice ▪

Find, circle, and write the words.

1.  s i h t <u>s k i n</u> h t m a u s c o r

   ➡

2.  h t i h s t o m a c h c k r s i u

   ➡

3. h u o s h n c k m h n a o h u r t

   ➡

⚙ Visualization   Cause & Effect

Use the words in the box to complete the chart.

water   dirty

Why?		**What Happened?**
The water is very _____ in Zambia.	⇨	Ayo is sick.
Ayo is sick.	⇨	Amara walks two miles to get _____ for Ayo.

UNIT 20 Science

How to Make Clean Water

▪ Words to Know ▪

Listen and repeat. 🎧

drink

cloth

charcoal

sand

rock

cap

top

slowly

How to Make Clean Water 🎧

You need to drink clean water.
This is how you can make clean water.

You need:

dirty water, a bottle, two pieces of cloth,
charcoal, sand, small rocks

1. Make 5 holes in the cap of the bottle.
2. Place a piece of cloth into the bottle.
3. Put some sand and small rocks on top.
4. Put charcoal on top.
5. Put another piece of cloth on top.
6. Slowly pour dirty water on top.
7. Soon, you'll have some clean water.

> 💬 **Key Expressions**
> A: How can I make clean water?
> B: Make 5 holes in the cap first.

▪ Comprehension Check ▪

Read and choose the correct answer.

1. What is the reading about?

　a. It's about how to drink clean water.

　b. It's about how to make clean water.

2. What is NOT needed to make clean water?

　a. clean water

　b. dirty water

3. You should make holes in the _____ of the bottle.

　a. cap　　　　　　**b.** cloth

▪ Sentence Focus ▪

Read and choose the correct sentence.

1.
　☐ Put a piece of cloth on top.
　☐ Put some small rocks on top.

2.
　☐ Put charcoal on top.
　☐ Put some sand on top.

3.
　☐ Make dirty water.
　☐ Pour dirty water.

Word Practice

Find, circle, and write the words.

1.  o k o k t r o k (d r i n k) t t k t

   →

2.  t o p p d o k r r c c o n p c k o

   →

3.  i k o o r c o d i o k r o c k n n

   →

☀ Visualization   Sequence

Use the words in the box to complete the chart. Then, number 1-4 to show the correct order.

| sand | charcoal |

		1	
Put _____ on top.	Slowly pour dirty water on top.	Place a piece of cloth into the bottle.	Put some _____ and small rocks on top.

UNIT 01

☐	**name**	이름
☐	**important**	중요한
☐	**part**	부분
☐	**mean**	의미하다
☐	**happy**	행복한
☐	**strong**	강한
☐	**princess**	공주
☐	**special**	특별한

UNIT 02

☐	**alphabet**	알파벳
☐	**start**	시작하다
☐	**end**	끝나다
☐	**between**	사이에
☐	**twenty**	20
☐	**twenty-six**	26
☐	**letter**	글자
☐	**guess**	짐작하다

UNIT 03

☐	**birthday**	생일
☐	**popsicle**	아이스캔디
☐	**doughnut**	도넛
☐	**stomachache**	배탈
☐	**sick**	아픈
☐	**party hat**	파티용 고깔모자
☐	**party horn**	파티용 나팔
☐	**friend**	친구

UNIT 04

☐	**gummy bear**	꼬마곰 젤리
☐	**soda**	탄산음료
☐	**mold**	아이스캔디 틀
☐	**fill**	채우다
☐	**pour**	붓다
☐	**poke**	(막대 등으로) 찌르다
☐	**freeze**	얼리다
☐	**enjoy**	즐기다

UNIT 05

☐	lost tooth	빠진 이
☐	pillow	베개
☐	blanket	담요
☐	dresser	서랍장
☐	curtain	커튼
☐	picture	사진
☐	clock	시계
☐	drawer	서랍

UNIT 06

☐	see	보다
☐	number	숫자
☐	man	남자
☐	woman	여자
☐	vase	꽃병
☐	pyramid	피라미드
☐	queen	여왕
☐	trick	속임수

UNIT 07

☐	late	늦은
☐	grab	움켜잡다
☐	push	밀다
☐	hurry	서두르다
☐	downstairs	아래층으로
☐	upstairs	위층으로
☐	put	넣다
☐	Sunday	일요일

UNIT 08

☐	eat	먹다
☐	breakfast	아침 식사
☐	fruit	과일
☐	noodle	국수
☐	pancake	팬케이크
☐	corn flakes	콘플레이크
☐	porridge	죽
☐	bread	빵

UNIT 09

☐	help	돕다
☐	plant	심다
☐	pick	따다
☐	make	만들다
☐	giraffe	기린
☐	snore	코를 골다
☐	corn	옥수수
☐	popcorn	팝콘

UNIT 10

☐	animal	동물
☐	sleep	자다
☐	day	낮
☐	night	밤
☐	a lot	많이
☐	little	거의 ~않는
☐	hour	시간
☐	human	사람

UNIT 11

☐	wet	젖은, 축축한
☐	dry	마른
☐	hot	더운
☐	cold	추운
☐	wind	바람
☐	cloudy	흐린
☐	rain	비가 오다
☐	change	변하다

UNIT 12

☐	tangram	칠교놀이
☐	puzzle	퍼즐
☐	triangle	삼각형
☐	square	사각형
☐	rectangle	직사각형
☐	people	사람들
☐	thing	물건
☐	quickly	빨리

UNIT 13

☐	bark	짖다
☐	hole	구멍
☐	search	찾아보다
☐	dig	파다
☐	snow	눈
☐	trapped	갇힌
☐	leap	뛰다
☐	wag	흔들다

UNIT 14

☐	hide	숨다
☐	hard	어려운
☐	caterpillar	애벌레
☐	branch	나뭇가지
☐	jaguar	재규어
☐	nest	둥지
☐	pattern	무늬
☐	wild	야생

UNIT 15

☐	weather	날씨
☐	Canada	캐나다
☐	winter	겨울
☐	carnival	축제
☐	dogsled racing	개썰매 경주
☐	snow tubing	튜브 눈썰매
☐	ice hotel	얼음 호텔
☐	visit	방문하다

UNIT 16

☐	local	현지의
☐	add	추가하다
☐	crab	게
☐	green salad	야채 샐러드
☐	grilled	구운
☐	drink	음료
☐	bottled water	병에 든 생수
☐	take-out	포장해 가는 음식

UNIT 17

☐	splash	첨벙거리다
☐	bath	욕조, 목욕
☐	bubble	거품
☐	wonder	궁금해하다
☐	sink	가라앉다
☐	float	뜨다
☐	tub	욕조
☐	soap	비누

UNIT 18

☐	look	보다
☐	desk	책상
☐	solid	고체
☐	liquid	액체
☐	gas	기체
☐	shape	모양
☐	size	크기
☐	matter	물질

UNIT 19

☐	dirty	더러운
☐	clean	깨끗한
☐	skin	피부
☐	stomach	배
☐	head	머리
☐	hurt	아프게 하다
☐	wake	일어나다
☐	get	얻다

UNIT 20

☐	drink	마시다
☐	cloth	천
☐	charcoal	숯
☐	sand	모래
☐	rock	돌
☐	cap	뚜껑
☐	top	위
☐	slowly	천천히

30만 독자가 선택한 초등 영작 교재

단어 블록 연결로
초등 문법과 영작을 동시에 해결!

기적의 영어문장 만들기 ❶~❺

주선이 지음 | 각 권 14,000원 | 초등 4~5학년 대상

---

1. 재미있는 역할극 만화로 문법 개념을 쉽게 이해해요.
2. 단어 블록을 조합하여 문장 어순을 한눈에 파악해요.
3. 뼈대 문장부터 긴 문장까지 단계적으로 직접 써 보며 훈련해요.

👆 추천 대상

☑ 단어는 많이 알지만 문장 완성은 자신이 없는 학생

☑ 주어나 시제에 따른 동사 사용에 실수가 많은 학생

☑ 고학년 대비 기초 문법을 익히고 싶은 학생

미국교과서 리딩 READING

2.1

READING

Workbook & Answer Key

길벗스쿨

미국교과서 리딩 READING

LEVEL 2 ①

Workbook

길벗스쿨

What's in Your Name?

Word Review

Ⓐ Choose and write.

name	mean	special	happy	important	part

1.

important

2.

3.

4.

5.

6.

Ⓑ Read and choose.

1. Bryan means 'strong.'

 b

2. Meena means 'princess.'

Sentence Review

A **Read and match.**

1.   What's in

    a makes you special!

2.   Your name

    b your name?

3.   Teresa means

    c 'happy.'

B **Unscramble and write.**

1. | is | Your | important. | name |

→ Your name is important.

2. | name | Her | Meena. | is |

→

3. | mean? | What | name | your | does |

→

UNIT 02 The Alphabet

Word Review

A Choose and write.

letter	between	twenty	end	start	twenty-six

1.
_____

2.
_____

3.
_____

4.
_____

5.
_____

6.
_____

B Read and choose.

1. The alphabet starts with ABC.
   ☐

2. Can you guess my name?
   ☐

Sentence Review

A **Read and match.**

1. There are
four letters

    a in my name.

2. My name ends

    b letters
all together.

3. That makes
twenty-six

    c with
the letter N.

B **Unscramble and write.**

1. | always | It | with | ends | XYZ. |

   →

2. | starts | My | with | name | the letter D. |

   →

3. | my | Can | you | name? | guess |

   →

UNIT 03

Happy Birthday!

Word Review

A Choose and write.

| doughnut   party horn   friend   birthday   party hat   stomachache |

1.

_____

2.

_____

3.

_____

4.

_____

5.

_____

6.

_____

B Read and choose.

1. I had a popsicle.

   ☐

2. Today, I am sick in bed.

   ☐

 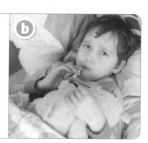

6

Sentence Review

A **Read and match.**

1.   Happy birthday   **a**   a doughnut.

2.   I have no   **b**   friends with me.

3.   I had   **c**   to me!

B **Unscramble and write.**

1. | Yesterday, | | went | | to | | I | | a party. |

    →

2. | have | | a party hat. | | I |

    →

3. | a stomachache! | | had | | I |

    →

Birthday Goodies

Word Review

A Choose and write.

| freeze | fill | poke | mold | soda | gummy bear |

1.

_____

2.

_____

3.

_____

4.

_____

5.

_____

6.

_____

B Read and choose.

1. Enjoy your popsicles!

[ ]

2. Pour soda in each mold.

[ ]

Sentence Review

A **Read and match.**

1. What you need:

2. Poke a popsicle stick

3. Fill molds

a. in the center of each mold.

b. with gummy bears.

c. gummy bears, mold, soda

B **Unscramble and write.**

1. | soda | in | Pour | each mold. |

    →

2. | molds | Fill | gummy bears. | with |

    →

3. | Gummy Bear Popsicles | make | Let's | for birthday! |

    →

UNIT 05

Where Is It?

Word Review

A **Choose and write.**

| blanket | dresser | picture | pillow | clock | drawer |

1.

_____

2.

_____

3.

_____

4.

_____

5.

_____

6.

_____

B **Read and choose.**

1. Is it behind his curtain? ☐

2. Where is his lost tooth? ☐

Sentence Review

A **Read and match.**

1.　　Is it

2.　　I have to

3.　　Is it between

a　look under the pillow.

b　his picture and clock?

c　under his blanket?

B **Unscramble and write.**

1.　| is | | Where | | lost tooth? | | Leo's |

　→

2.　| on | | it | | Is | | dresser? | | his |

　→

3.　| his | | in | | Oh, | | it | | hand! | | was |

　→

UNIT 06

Your Eyes Play Tricks

Word Review

A Choose and write.

| man | number | vase | woman | pyramid | trick |

1.
_____

2.
_____

3.
_____

4.
_____

5.
_____

6.
_____

B Read and choose.

1. What do you see? ☐

2. Sometimes, you see a queen of Egypt. ☐

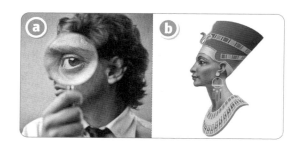

Sentence Review

A **Read and match.**

1. Sometimes, you see

2. What do

3. Look closely

a. at these pictures.

b. numbers.

c. you see?

B **Unscramble and write.**

1. | letters. | Sometimes, | see | you |

    →

2. | But | see | you | a vase. | sometimes, |

    →

3. | play | eyes | Your | tricks! |

    →

I Am Late!

Word Review

A **Choose and write.**

| grab | put | hurry | push | downstairs | upstairs |

1.

_____

2.

_____

3.

_____

4.

_____

5.

_____

6.

_____

B **Read and choose.**

1. It's <u>Sunday</u> today!

   ☐

2. I got up late for school!

   ☐

Sentence Review

A **Read and match.**

1.   I hurry

2.   I grab

3.   I quickly put

a   my bag.

b   downstairs.

c   my books in my bag.

B **Unscramble and write.**

1. | my | | I | | books! | | forgot |

→

2. | upstairs. | | I | | go back |

→

3. | bedroom door | | open. | | I | | push | | my |

→

UNIT 08

What's for Breakfast?

Word Review

A **Choose and write.**

| bread | pancake | porridge | eat | noodle | fruit |

1.

_____

2.

_____

3.

_____

4.

_____

5.

_____

6.

_____

B **Read and choose.**

1. Every kid eats breakfast! ☐

2. Some kids eat corn flakes for breakfast. ☐

Sentence Review

A Read and match.

1. Kids around the world

2. Some kids eat

3. Some kids eat fruit

a. bread for breakfast.

b. eat breakfast.

c. for breakfast.

B Unscramble and write.

1. | kids | What | eat | do | for breakfast? |

→

2. | eat | Some | for breakfast. | kids | noodles |

→

3. | for breakfast. | Some | eat | kids | pancakes |

→

Who Will Help Me?

Word Review

A Choose and write.

| corn | make | giraffe | help | plant | snore |

1. _____

2. _____

3. _____

4. _____

5. _____

6. _____

B Read and choose.

1. Who will help me pick the corn? ☐

2. Who will help me make popcorn? ☐

18

Sentence Review

A **Read and match.**

1.   Who will help me

2.   "Not we," said

3.   "We will,"

a   said Cat and Dog.

b   plant corn?

c   Cat and Dog.

B **Unscramble and write.**

1. | Who | me | pick | will help | the corn? |

→

2. | "Zzzzz..." | Cat | snored | and Dog. |

→

3. | eat | the popcorn? | Who | will help | me |

→

Animals' Sleep

Word Review

A Choose and write.

animal	night	little	a lot	hour	human

1.

_____

2.

_____

3.

_____

4.

_____

5.

_____

6.

_____

B Read and choose.

1. Some animals sleep during the day. ☐

2. How much do animals sleep? ☐

Sentence Review

A **Read and match.**

1. This animal sleeps

2. Some animals

3. Some animals sleep during

a the night.

b 12.1 hours a day.

c sleep a lot.

B **Unscramble and write.**

1. | sleep | 8 hours | a day. | I |

   →

2. | sleep | Some | very | animals | little. |

   →

3. | This | sleeps | animal | a day. | 14.4 hours |

   →

Weather

Word Review

A **Choose and write.**

| dry | rain | wet | change | cold | hot |

1.

2.

3.

4.

5.

6.

B **Read and choose.**

1. It was <u>cloudy</u> in the morning. ☐

2. Now, we have a strong <u>wind</u>. ☐

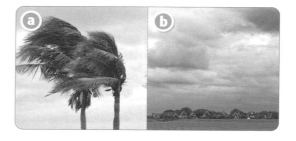

ⓐ ⓑ

Sentence Review

A Read and match.

1. How hot or

2. Can you see

3. Look out

a. the window.

b. the sun?

c. cold is it?

B Unscramble and write.

1. | changes | The weather | all the time. |

   →

2. | wet | it | Is | or dry? |

   →

3. | there | Are | clouds? |

   →

Let's Play with Tangrams

Word Review

A Choose and write.

| puzzle | thing | quickly | triangle | rectangle | square |

1.

_____

2.

_____

3.

_____

4.

_____

5.

_____

6.

_____

B Read and choose.

1. A tangram is a Chinese puzzle.
   [ ]

2. You can make shapes of people.
   [ ]

24

Sentence Review

A **Read and match.**

1. You can make

2. It is

3. Do you want

ⓐ raining outside.

ⓑ shapes of things.

ⓒ to play, too?

B **Unscramble and write.**

1. | make? | can | you | What |

   →

2. | shapes | You | of animals. | can | make |

   →

3. | a perfect day | is | It | with a tangram. | to play |

   →

UNIT 13

What a Team!

Word Review

Ⓐ Choose and write.

wag	trapped	snow	hole	search	leap

1.

_____

2.

_____

3.

_____

4.

_____

5.

_____

6.

_____

Ⓑ Read and choose.

1. Kevin barks at a hole.

☐

2. Kevin quickly digs the hole bigger.

☐

Sentence Review

A **Read and match.**

1.   I pet

2.   Kevin leaps and

3.   I pull out the man

ⓐ   trapped in snow.

ⓑ   Kevin.

ⓒ   wags his tail.

B **Unscramble and write.**

1. | run | I | Kevin. | to |

    →

2. | "Search!" | Kevin | give | I | the order |

    →

3. | a good | make | team! | We |

    →

UNIT 14 Camouflage

Word Review

A Choose and write.

pattern	wild	branch	hard	hide	caterpillar

1.

_____

2.

_____

3.

_____

4.

_____

5.

_____

6.

_____

B Read and choose.

1. This jaguar is hard to see in the trees.

2. These eggs are hard to see in the nest.

 a
 b

Sentence Review

A **Read and match.**

1. This caterpillar is

2. These birds are hard

3. How do animals

a) hard to see on a branch.

b) hide in the wild?

c) to see in the grass.

B **Unscramble and write.**

1. in the sand. | to see | hard | This fish | is

   →

2. These snakes | hard | to see | are | in the tree.

   →

3. use | Animals | colors | or patterns | to hide.

   →

Winter Carnival

Word Review

A **Choose and write.**

| weather | carnival | winter | Canada | ice hotel | dogsled racing |

1.

_____

2.

_____

3.

_____

4.

_____

5.

_____

6.

_____

B **Read and choose.**

1. You should visit here!

2. I enjoyed snow tubing.

Sentence Review

A **Read and match.**

1. The weather is

2. I enjoyed staying

3. I'm writing to you

a) in an ice hotel.

b) from Quebec, Canada.

c) cold and snowy.

B **Unscramble and write.**

1. | I | the Québec Winter Carnival. | visited |

→

2. | I | dogsled racing. | enjoyed |

→

3. | like | it | I | in Quebec. | here |

→

What's for Lunch?

Word Review

A Choose and write.

crab	grilled	local	drink	add	green salad

1.

_____

2.

_____

3.

_____

4.

_____

5.

_____

6.

_____

B Read and choose.

1. "TAKE-OUT AVAILABLE"

   ☐

2. I want the <u>bottled water</u>.

   ☐

Sentence Review

A Read and match.

1. What's for

2. I want

3. I need $3 to

a drink an orange juice.

b the green salad.

c lunch?

B Unscramble and write.

1. | for lunch? | | do | | What | | you | | want |

    →

2. | want | | the local salmon. | | I |

    →

3. | a large soda. | | need | | $2 | | to drink | | I |

    →

Will It Sink or Float?

Word Review

A Choose and write.

| sink | tub | soap | wonder | bath | splash |

1.

2.

3.

4.

5.

6.

B Read and choose.

1. He can make some bubbles.

2. Will it sink or will it float?

Sentence Review

A **Read and match.**

1. Will the soap

2. Andy puts them

3. He can

(a) sink or float?

(b) quack.

(c) in the tub.

B **Unscramble and write.**

1. | Andy's | He | bath time | is | friend. |

    →

2. | loves | Andy | in the bath. | to splash |

    →

3. | it | Will | sink | or float? |

    →

UNIT 18

Discover Matter

Word Review

A Choose and write.

solid	desk	shape	gas	size	matter

1. _____

2. _____

3. _____

4. _____

5. _____

6. _____

B Read and choose.

1. Milk is a <u>liquid</u>.

2. <u>Look</u> all around.

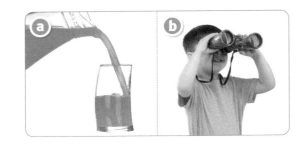

Sentence Review

(A) **Read and match.**

1.   A solid has

2.   Air in the ball

3.   Solids, liquids, and gases

(a) are matter.

(b) a shape.

(c) is a gas.

(B) **Unscramble and write.**

1. | matter. | is | A desk |

→

2. | change | A gas | can | and size. | shape |

→

3. | can | A liquid | shape. | change |

→

The Story of Ayo

Word Review

A Choose and write.

clean	head	dirty	hurt	stomach	get

1. _____

2.  _____

3.  _____

4. _____

5.  _____

6.  _____

B Read and choose.

1. It makes Ayo's skin hurt.
   ☐

2. Amara wakes up before the sun.
   ☐

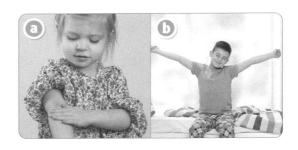

Sentence Review

A **Read and match.**

1. It makes

2. She lives with

3. Ayo feels

a her sister, Amara.

b sorry for Amara.

c Ayo's stomach hurt.

B **Unscramble and write.**

1. | is | dirty | The water | in Zambia. | very |

   →

2. | Ayo's | makes | It | hurt. | head |

   →

3. | to get | She | walks | two miles | water. |

   →

How to Make Clean Water

Word Review

A Choose and write.

| rock | top | sand | charcoal | cloth | slowly |

1. _____

2. _____

3. _____

4. _____

5. _____

6. _____

B Read and choose.

1. You need to drink clean water. ☐

2. Make 5 holes in the cap of the bottle. ☐

ⓐ   ⓑ

Sentence Review

A **Read and match.**

1. Put charcoal

2. Soon, you'll

3. Slowly pour

a. dirty water on top.

b. have some clean water.

c. on top.

B **Unscramble and write.**

1. | can | I | How | clean water? | make |

→

2. | Place | into the bottle. | a piece of | cloth |

→

3. | some sand | on top. | Put | and small rocks |

→

Unit 01. What's in Your Name?

Word Review Ⓑ **1.** ⓑ **2.** ⓐ

Sentence Review

Ⓐ **1.** ⓑ **2.** ⓐ **3.** ⓒ

Ⓑ **1.** Your name is important.
2. Her name is Meena.
3. What does your name mean?

Unit 02. The Alphabet

Word Review Ⓑ **1.** ⓑ **2.** ⓐ

Sentence Review

Ⓐ **1.** ⓐ **2.** ⓒ **3.** ⓑ

Ⓑ **1.** It always ends with XYZ.
2. My name starts with the letter D.
3. Can you guess my name?

Unit 03. Happy Birthday!

Word Review Ⓑ **1.** ⓐ **2.** ⓑ

Sentence Review

Ⓐ **1.** ⓒ **2.** ⓑ **3.** ⓐ

Ⓑ **1.** Yesterday, I went to a party.
2. I have a party hat.
3. I had a stomachache!

Unit 04. Birthday Goodies

Word Review Ⓑ **1.** ⓐ **2.** ⓑ

Sentence Review

Ⓐ **1.** ⓒ **2.** ⓐ **3.** ⓑ

Ⓑ **1.** Pour soda in each mold.
2. Fill molds with gummy bears.
3. Let's make Gummy Bear Popsicles for birthday!

Unit 05. Where Is It?

Word Review Ⓑ **1.** ⓑ **2.** ⓐ

Sentence Review

Ⓐ **1.** ⓒ **2.** ⓐ **3.** ⓑ

Ⓑ **1.** Where is Leo's lost tooth?
2. Is it on his dresser?
3. Oh, it was in his hand!

Unit 06. Your Eyes Play Tricks

Word Review Ⓑ **1.** ⓐ **2.** ⓑ

Sentence Review

Ⓐ **1.** ⓑ **2.** ⓒ **3.** ⓐ

Ⓑ **1.** Sometimes, you see letters.
2. But sometimes, you see a vase.
3. Your eyes play tricks!

Unit 07. I Am Late!

Word Review Ⓑ **1.** ⓑ **2.** ⓐ

Sentence Review

Ⓐ **1.** ⓑ **2.** ⓐ **3.** ⓒ

Ⓑ **1.** I forgot my books!
2. I go back upstairs.
3. I push my bedroom door open.

Unit 08. What's for Breakfast?

Word Review　Ⓑ **1.** ⓐ　**2.** ⓑ

Sentence Review

Ⓐ **1.** ⓑ　**2.** ⓐ　**3.** ⓒ

Ⓑ **1.** What do kids eat for breakfast?
　　2. Some kids eat noodles for breakfast.
　　3. Some kids eat pancakes for breakfast.

Unit 09. Who Will Help Me?

Word Review　Ⓑ **1.** ⓐ　**2.** ⓑ

Sentence Review

Ⓐ **1.** ⓑ　**2.** ⓒ　**3.** ⓐ

Ⓑ **1.** Who will help me pick the corn?
　　2. "Zzzzz…" snored Cat and Dog.
　　3. Who will help me eat the popcorn?

Unit 10. Animals' Sleep

Word Review　Ⓑ **1.** ⓐ　**2.** ⓑ

Sentence Review

Ⓐ **1.** ⓑ　**2.** ⓒ　**3.** ⓐ

Ⓑ **1.** I sleep 8 hours a day.
　　2. Some animals sleep very little.
　　3. This animal sleeps 14.4 hours a day.

Unit 11. Weather

Word Review　Ⓑ **1.** ⓑ　**2.** ⓐ

Sentence Review

Ⓐ **1.** ⓒ　**2.** ⓑ　**3.** ⓐ

Ⓑ **1.** The weather changes all the time.
　　2. Is it wet or dry?
　　3. Are there clouds?

Unit 12. Let's Play with Tangrams

Word Review　Ⓑ **1.** ⓐ　**2.** ⓑ

Sentence Review

Ⓐ **1.** ⓑ　**2.** ⓐ　**3.** ⓒ

Ⓑ **1.** What can you make?
　　2. You can make shapes of animals.
　　3. It is a perfect day to play with a
　　　tangram.

Unit 13. What a Team!

Word Review　Ⓑ **1.** ⓑ　**2.** ⓐ

Sentence Review

Ⓐ **1.** ⓑ　**2.** ⓒ　**3.** ⓐ

Ⓑ **1.** I run to Kevin.
　　2. I give Kevin the order "Search!"
　　3. We make a good team!

Unit 14. Camouflage

Word Review　Ⓑ **1.** ⓑ　**2.** ⓐ

Sentence Review

Ⓐ **1.** ⓐ　**2.** ⓒ　**3.** ⓑ

Ⓑ **1.** This fish is hard to see in the sand.
　　2. These snakes are hard to see in the
　　　tree.
　　3. Animals use colors or patterns to hide.

Unit 15. Winter Carnival

Word Review　Ⓑ **1.** ⓐ　**2.** ⓑ

Sentence Review

Ⓐ **1.** ⓒ　**2.** ⓐ　**3.** ⓑ

Ⓑ **1.** I visited the Québec Winter Carnival.
　　2. I enjoyed dogsled racing.
　　3. I like it here in Québec.

Unit 16. What's for Lunch?

Word Review B 1. ⓑ 2. ⓐ

Sentence Review

A 1. ⓒ 2. ⓑ 3. ⓐ

B 1. What do you want for lunch?
2. I want the local salmon.
3. I need $2 to drink a large soda.

Unit 17. Will It Sink or Float?

Word Review B 1. ⓑ 2. ⓐ

Sentence Review

A 1. ⓐ 2. ⓒ 3. ⓑ

B 1. He is Andy's bath time friend.
2. Andy loves to splash in the bath.
3. Will it sink or float?

Unit 18. Discover Matter

Word Review B 1. ⓐ 2. ⓑ

Sentence Review

A 1. ⓑ 2. ⓒ 3. ⓐ

B 1. A desk is matter.
2. A gas can change shape and size.
3. A liquid can change shape.

Unit 19. The Story of Ayo

Word Review B 1. ⓐ 2. ⓑ

Sentence Review

A 1. ⓒ 2. ⓐ 3. ⓑ

B 1. The water is very dirty in Zambia.
2. It makes Ayo's head hurt.
3. She walks two miles to get water.

Unit 20. How to Make Clean Water

Word Review B 1. ⓐ 2. ⓑ

Sentence Review

A 1. ⓒ 2. ⓑ 3. ⓐ

B 1. How can I make clean water?
2. Place a piece of cloth into the bottle.
3. Put some sand and small rocks on top.

미국교과서 리딩

READING

LEVEL 2 ①

Answer Key

길벗스쿨

Talk About It

- 당신의 이름은 무엇인가요?
- 당신은 당신의 이름을 좋아하나요?

Words to Know

듣고 따라 말해 보세요.

- name 이름
- part 부분
- happy 행복한
- princess 공주
- important 중요한
- mean 의미하다
- strong 강한
- special 특별한

Main Reading

당신의 이름 속에는 무엇이 있나요?

당신의 이름 속에는 무엇이 있나요? 당신의 이름은 중요해요. 그것은 당신의 일부니까요. 당신의 이름은 무슨 뜻인가요? 그녀의 이름은 테레사예요. 테레사는 행복하다는 뜻이에요. 그의 이름은 브라이언이에요. 브라이언은 강하다는 뜻이에요. 그녀의 이름은 미나예요. 미나는 공주라는 뜻이에요. 당신의 이름은 당신을 특별하게 해 줘요!

- 테레사는 중국어로 '행복한'이라는 뜻이에요.
- 브라이언은 영어로 '강한'이라는 뜻이에요.
- 미나는 힌두어로 '공주'라는 뜻이에요.

Key Expressions

A: 네 이름은 무슨 뜻이야?
B: 내 이름은 '행복한'이라는 뜻이야.

| 문제 정답 및 해설 |

Comprehension Check

읽고 알맞은 답을 고르세요.

1. 무엇에 관한 글인가요? [정답 : b]
   a. 재미있는 이름에 관한 글이에요.
   b. 이름이 왜 중요한지에 관한 글이에요.

2. 브라이언이라는 이름은 무슨 뜻인가요? [정답 : a]
   a. '강한'이라는 뜻이에요.
   b. '공주'라는 뜻이에요.

3. 당신의 이름은 당신을 특별하게 해 줘요. [정답 : a]
   a. 특별한
   b. 행복한

Sentence Focus

읽고 알맞은 문장을 고르세요.

1. ■ 그녀의 이름은 테레사예요.
   □ 그녀의 이름은 미나예요.

2. □ 그의 이름은 미나예요.
   ■ 그의 이름은 브라이언이에요.

3. □ 테레사는 '행복한'이라는 뜻이에요.
   ■ 미나는 '공주'라는 뜻이에요.

Word Practice

그림에 알맞은 단어를 찾아 동그라미 하고, 써 보세요.

1. ⓢⓟⓔⓒⓘⓐⓛ p c t a a e r n s c [special]
2. e a n c ⓟⓐⓡⓣ e r s r l m n e m [part]
3. s ⓝⓐⓜⓔ i l a c i p a e c p n a [name]

Visualization : 원인과 결과

주어진 단어를 이용해서 표를 완성하세요.

- (순서대로) name / special
- 나의 이름은 나의 일부예요. ⇨ 나의 이름은 중요해요.
- 나의 이름에는 의미가 있어요.
  ⇨ 나의 이름은 나를 특별하게 해요.

Talk About It

- 알파벳에 대해 무엇을 알고 있나요?
- 알파벳 노래를 부를 수 있나요?

Words to Know

듣고 따라 말해 보세요.

- alphabet 알파벳
- end 끝나다
- twenty 20
- letter 글자
- start 시작하다
- between 사이에
- twenty-six 26
- guess 짐작하다

Main Reading

알파벳

알파벳은 ABC로 시작해요. 그리고 언제나 XYZ로 끝나요. 그리고 그 사이에는 스무 개의 다른 글자들이 있어요. 그래서 모두 다 합치면 스물여섯 개의 글자가 되어요. 내 이름에는 네 개의 글자가 있어요. 내 이름은 D로 시작해요. 내 이름은 N으로 끝나요. 내 이름을 알아맞힐 수 있나요?

Key Expressions

A: 네 이름은 무엇으로 시작하니?
B: 내 이름은 R로 시작해.

| 문제 정답 및 해설 |

Comprehension Check

읽고 알맞은 답을 고르세요.

1. 무엇에 관한 글인가요? 　　　　　　　　　　　[정답 : b]
　a. 숫자에 관한 글이에요.
　b. 알파벳에 관한 글이에요.

2. 알파벳에는 몇 개의 글자가 있나요? 　　　　　　[정답 : b]
　a. 스무 개의 글자가 있어요.
　b. 스물여섯 개의 글자가 있어요.

3. 내 이름은 <u>Dain</u>이에요. 　　　　　　　　　[정답 : b]
　a. Dan (댄)
　b. Dain (다인)

Sentence Focus

읽고 알맞은 문장을 고르세요.

1. ■ 알파벳은 ABC로 시작해요.
　　□ 알파벳은 XYZ로 시작해요.

2. □ 내 이름은 글자 D로 끝나요.
　　■ 내 이름은 글자 N으로 끝나요.

3. ■ 내 이름에는 네 개의 글자가 있어요.
　　□ 내 이름에는 스물여섯 개의 글자가 있어요.

Word Practice

그림에 알맞은 단어를 찾아 동그라미 하고, 써 보세요.

1. e e e s u l e g n e t e (g u e s s) 　　　[guess]
2. n e e b w e (b e t w e e n) e e g 　　　[between]
3. r t n e t e t e (l e t t e r) n n s 　　　[letter]

Visualization : 주제와 세부사항

주어진 단어를 이용해서 표를 완성하세요.

- (순서대로) <u>starts</u> / <u>ends</u>
- 주제 – 알파벳
- 세부사항 – 그것은 ABC로 시작해요.
　　　　　　　그것은 XYZ로 끝나요.

Talk About It

- 당신의 생일은 언제인가요?
- 당신은 생일에 무엇을 하나요?

Words to Know

듣고 따라 말해 보세요.

- birthday 생일
- doughnut 도넛
- sick 아픈
- party horn 파티용 나팔
- popsicle 아이스캔디
- stomacheache 배탈
- party hat 파티용 고깔모자
- friend 친구

Main Reading

생일 축하해!

어제 나는 파티에 다녀왔어. 아이스캔디를 먹었어. 도넛도 먹었고. 케이크도 먹었어. 그랬더니 배탈이 났지 뭐야! 오늘은 아파서 침대에 누워 있어. 파티용 고깔모자가 있고. 파티용 나팔도 있지. 하지만 내 곁엔 친구들이 없어. 내 스스로의 생일을 축하해!

- 방문객 금지
- 곧 나으렴!

Key Expressions

- 나는 아이스캔디를 먹었어.
- 나는 파티용 고깔모자를 가지고 있어.

| 문제 정답 및 해설 |

Comprehension Check

읽고 알맞은 답을 고르세요.

1. 오늘은 어떤 특별한 날인가요? [정답 : a]
   a. 오늘은 내 생일이에요.
   b. 오늘은 크리스마스예요.

2. 나는 오늘 어떤가요? [정답 : b]
   a. 집에서 즐겁게 있어요.
   b. 아파서 침대에 누워 있어요.

3. 오늘 내 곁에 친구들이 없어요. [정답 : a]
   a. 친구들
   b. 파티용 고깔모자들

Sentence Focus

읽고 알맞은 문장을 고르세요.

1. ■ 나는 도넛을 먹었어요.
   □ 나는 케이크를 먹었어요.

2. ■ 나는 아이스캔디를 먹었어요.
   □ 나는 배탈이 났어요.

3. □ 나는 파티용 고깔모자를 가지고 있어요.
   ■ 나는 파티용 나팔을 가지고 있어요.

Word Practice

그림에 알맞은 단어를 찾아 동그라미 하고, 써 보세요.

1. y i t y t o o s (s i c k) p h e r p [sick]
2. h p e h y a (p o p s i c l e) c i i [popsicle]
3. t (p a r t y h a t) p p s s s i i s [party hat]

Visualization : 원인과 결과

주어진 단어를 이용해서 표를 완성하세요.

- (순서대로) stomachache / birthday

왜인가요?	무슨 일이 일어났나요?
· 아이스캔디를 먹었어요. 도넛도 먹었어요. 케이크도 먹었어요.	⇨ 배탈이 났어요.
· 오늘은 내 생일이에요.	⇨ 나는 파티용 고깔모자와 파티용 나팔을 가지고 있어요.

Talk About It

· 생일에 먹는 맛있는 것들에는 무엇이 있나요?
· 당신은 아이스캔디를 좋아하나요?

Words to Know

듣고 따라 말해 보세요.

· gummy bear 꼬마곰 젤리
· mold 아이스캔디 틀
· pour 붓다
· freeze 얼리다
· soda 탄산음료
· fill 채우다
· poke (막대 등으로) 찌르다
· enjoy 즐기다

Main Reading

생일에 먹는 맛있는 것들

생일에 먹는 꼬마곰 젤리 아이스캔디를 만들어요!

준비물: 꼬마곰 젤리, 틀, 탄산음료

만드는 방법 :

1. 꼬마곰 젤리로 틀을 채워요.
2. 각각의 틀에 탄산음료를 부어요.
3. 틀 가운데에 아이스캔디 막대를 꽂아요.
4. 적어도 다섯 시간 동안 얼려요.
5. 완성된 당신의 아이스캔디를 맛있게 먹어요!

Key Expressions

A: 각각의 틀에 탄산음료를 부어.
B: 알겠어.

| 문제 정답 및 해설 |

Comprehension Check

읽고 알맞은 답을 고르세요.

1. 무엇에 관한 글인가요? [정답 : b]
   a. 아이스캔디를 먹는 법에 관한 글이에요.
   b. 아이스캔디를 만드는 법에 관한 글이에요.

2. 아이스캔디를 만들 때 무엇이 필요한가요? [정답 : b]

   a. 곰이 필요해요.
   b. 아이스캔디 틀이 필요해요.

3. 적어도 <u>다섯</u> 시간 동안 기다려야 해요. [정답 : a]
   a. 다섯
   b. 아홉

Sentence Focus

읽고 알맞은 문장을 고르세요.

1. ■ 틀에 꼬마곰 젤리를 채워요.
   □ 틀에 탄산음료를 채워요.

2. □ 각각의 틀에 탄산음료를 꽂아요.
   ■ 각각의 틀에 탄산음료를 부어요.

3. □ 각각의 틀 가운데에서 아이스캔디 막대를 찾아내요.
   ■ 각각의 틀 가운데에 아이스캔디 막대를 꽂아요.

Word Practice

그림에 알맞은 단어를 찾아 동그라미 하고, 써 보세요.

1. j j e f s s s e n e (e n j o y) d a [enjoy]
2. e o a (f r e e z e) y a s n y y z e [freeze]
3. s o (s o d a) f e f o e n d o r a j [soda]

Visualization : 순서

주어진 단어를 이용해서 표를 완성하세요. 그리고 올바른 순서에 따라 1-4를 써 보세요.

· (순서대로) <u>Poke</u> / <u>Fill</u>
· 3 각각의 틀에 아이스캔디 막대를 <u>꽂아요</u>.
  2 각각의 틀에 탄산음료를 부어요.
  1 틀에 꼬마곰 젤리를 <u>채워요</u>.
  4 적어도 다섯 시간 동안 얼려요.

Talk About It

- 당신의 치아는 몇 개인가요?
- 당신의 치아 중에 흔들리는 이가 있나요?

Words to Know

듣고 따라 말해 보세요.

- lost tooth 빠진 이
- pillow 베개
- blanket 담요
- dresser 서랍장
- curtain 커튼
- picture 사진
- clock 시계
- drawer 서랍

Main Reading

어디에 있지?

나는 첫 번째로 빠진 레오의 이를 가지러 왔어. 베개 밑부터 살펴봐야겠어. 앗! 레오의 빠진 이는 어디에 있지? 레오의 담요 밑에 있나? 서랍장 위에 있나? 서랍 속에 있나? 레오의 사진과 시계 사이에 있는 걸까? 커튼 뒤에 있으려나? 레오의 빠진 이는 어디에 있는 거지? 아, 레오의 손에 있었구나!

Key Expressions

A: 레오의 빠진 이는 어디에 있지?
B: 그의 손에 있어.

| 문제 정답 및 해설 |

Comprehension Check

읽고 알맞은 답을 고르세요.

1. 나는 누구인가요? [정답 : b]
   a. 나는 레오예요.
   b. 나는 이빨 요정이에요.

2. 레오의 빠진 이는 어디에 있었나요? [정답 : b]
   a. 그의 서랍 안에 있었어요.
   b. 그의 손에 있었어요.

3. 나는 첫번째로 빠진 레오의 이를 가지러 왔어요. [정답 : a]
   a. 첫 번째
   b. 두 번째

Sentence Focus

읽고 알맞은 문장을 고르세요.

1. □ 침대 밑을 살펴봐야겠어요.
   ■ 담요 밑을 살펴봐야겠어요.

2. ■ 서랍장 위에 있나요?
   □ 커튼 뒤에 있나요?

3. ■ 그의 빠진 이는 어디에 있을까요?
   □ 그의 잃어버린 시계는 어디에 있을까요?

Word Practice

그림에 알맞은 단어를 찾아 동그라미 하고, 써 보세요.

1. e c o i c e clock t u c p t u [clock]
2. u c c k c t u l c c picture [picture]
3. r t curtain a e k r u t k l [curtain]

Visualization : 문제와 해결책

주어진 단어를 이용해서 표를 완성하세요.

- (순서대로) lost tooth / dresser

문제	해결책
· 레오의 빠진 이는 어디에 있나요?	⇨ 베개 밑을 살펴봐야해요.
	⇨ 서랍장 위를 살펴봐야해요.

Talk About It

- 그림에서 무엇이 보이나요?
- 원이 움직이고 있다고 생각하나요?

Words to Know

듣고 따라 말해 보세요.

- see 보다
- man 남자
- vase 꽃병
- queen 여왕
- number 숫자
- woman 여자
- pyramid 피라미드
- trick 속임수

Main Reading

여러분의 눈은 속임수를 쓴답니다

여기에 있는 그림들을 잘 살펴보세요. 무엇이 보이나요? 때로 여러분은 글자를 볼 거예요. 또 때로는 숫자를 보게 되죠. 때로는 남자와 여자가 보일 거예요. 때로는 꽃병이 보이고요. 때로 여러분은 피라미드 사이에 있는 한 남자를 볼 거예요. 하지만 때로는 이집트 여왕을 보게 되죠. 가끔은 여러분이 보고 있다고 생각하는 것이 사실은 아닙니다. 여러분의 눈은 속임수를 쓰니까요!

Key Expressions

A: 그림에서 무엇이 보이니?
B: 때로 나는 토끼를 봐.

| 문제 정답 및 해설 |

Comprehension Check

읽고 알맞은 답을 고르세요.

1. 무엇에 관한 글인가요?　　　　　　　　　　[정답 : b]
　a. 생각하는 방법에 관한 글이에요.
　b. 보는 것에 관한 글이에요.

2. 왜 여러분은 때때로 전체 그림을 보지 못하나요?　[정답 : a]
　a. 내 눈이 속임수를 쓰기 때문이에요.
　b. 내 시력이 나쁘기 때문이에요.

3. 가끔은 여러분이 보고 있다고 생각하는 것이 사실은 아닙니다.
　a. 사진　　　　　　　　　　　　　　　　[정답 : b]
　b. 사실

Sentence Focus

읽고 알맞은 문장을 고르세요.

1. □ 때로 나는 남자를 봐요.
　■ 때로 나는 여왕을 봐요.

2. □ 이 피라미드들을 잘 살펴보세요.
　■ 이 숫자들을 잘 살펴보세요.

3. ■ 여러분의 눈은 속임수를 써요!
　□ 여러분의 친구들은 속임수를 써요!

Word Practice

그림에 알맞은 단어를 찾아 동그라미 하고, 써 보세요.

1. n(man)nnmiaornknawk　　　　　[man]
2. imtmckiinat(woman)i　　　　　[woman]
3. anookwaocw(trick)ac　　　　　[trick]

Visualization : 원인과 결과

주어진 단어를 이용해서 표를 완성하세요.

- (순서대로) tricks / letters

왜인가요?	무슨 일이 일어났나요?
· 여러분의 눈은 속임수를 써요.	⇨ 때로 나는 글자를 봐요.
	⇨ 하지만 때로는 숫자를 봐요.

Talk About It

- 당신은 몇 시에 일어나나요?
- 학교 수업은 몇 시에 시작하나요?

Words to Know

듣고 따라 말해 보세요.

- late 늦은
- push 밀다
- downstairs 아래층으로
- put 넣다
- grab 움켜잡다
- hurry 서두르다
- upstairs 위층으로
- Sunday 일요일

Main Reading

지각이야!

아니, 이런! 늦잠을 자서 학교에 지각이야! 나는 가방을 잽싸게 집어 들어. 내 침실 문을 밀어서 열지. 그리고 서둘러 계단을 내려가. 아니, 이럴 수가! 책을 놓고 와버렸잖아! 나는 다시 계단을 올라가. 재빨리 책을 가방에 던져 넣지. 나는 다시 계단을 내려가. "오늘은 일요일이야, 론!" 엄마가 말씀하시네. 깜박했다! 오늘은 일요일이야!

Key Expressions

A: 늦잠을 자서 학교에 지각이야.
B: 오늘은 일요일이야.

| 문제 정답 및 해설 |

Comprehension Check

읽고 알맞은 답을 고르세요.

1. 나는 왜 서두르나요?   [정답 : a]
  a. 늦잠을 자서 학교에 지각했기 때문이에요.
  b. 책을 두고 왔기 때문이에요.

2. 오늘은 무슨 요일인가요?   [정답 : a]
  a. 오늘은 일요일이에요.
  b. 오늘은 학교 가는 날이에요.

3. 나는 위층으로 다시 올라가 책을 가방에 넣어요.   [정답 : b]
  a. 밀다
  b. 넣다

Sentence Focus

읽고 알맞은 문장을 고르세요.

1. ■ 나는 문을 밀어요.
  □ 나는 가방을 밀어요.

2. □ 나는 계단을 다시 올라가요.
  ■ 나는 계단을 다시 내려가요.

3. ■ 나는 가방에 책을 넣어요.
  □ 나는 가방에 신발을 넣어요.

Word Practice

그림에 알맞은 단어를 찾아 동그라미 하고, 써 보세요.

1. h l l late t r r y t p a u h l   [late]
2. r y a hurry r l u p u t p y l   [hurry]
3. a y t p a a a p r y a t put e h   [put]

Visualization : 배경

주어진 단어를 이용해서 표를 완성하세요.

- (왼쪽부터) push / Sunday
- 무엇을? – 가방을 잽싸게 집어 들어요.
  – 내 침실 문을 밀어서 열어요.
  – 서둘러 계단을 내려가요.
  – 다시 계단을 올라가요.
- 언제? – 오늘은 일요일이에요.

Talk About It

- 당신은 매일 아침에 아침 식사를 하나요?
- 아침 식사로 무엇을 먹고 싶은가요?

Words to Know

듣고 따라 말해 보세요.

- eat 먹다
- fruit 과일
- pancake 팬케이크
- porridge 죽
- breakfast 아침 식사
- noodle 국수
- corn flakes 콘플레이크
- bread 빵

Main Reading

아침 식사로 무엇을 먹나요?

전 세계에 있는 어린이들은 아침 식사를 해요. 어떤 어린이들은 아침 식사로 과일을 먹어요. 어떤 어린이들은 아침 식사로 국수를 먹어요. 또 어떤 어린이들은 아침 식사로 팬케이크를 먹지요. 어떤 어린이들은 아침 식사로 콘플레이크를 먹습니다. 어떤 어린이들은 아침 식사로 죽을 먹어요. 또 어떤 어린이들은 아침 식사로 빵을 먹지요. 모든 어린이들은 아침 식사를 해요!

(왼쪽부터 시계방향으로)

- 브라질 : 과일
- 미국 : 팬케이크
- 러시아 : 죽
- 이집트 : 피타빵
- 베트남 : 국수
- 호주 : 콘플레이크

Key Expressions

A: 어린이들은 아침 식사로 무엇을 먹니?
B: 어떤 어린이들은 과일을 먹어.

| 문제 정답 및 해설 |

Comprehension Check

읽고 알맞은 답을 고르세요.

1. 무엇에 관한 글인가요? [정답 : b]
   a. 어린이들에 관한 글이에요.
   b. 아침 식사에 관한 글이에요.

2. 어린이들은 아침 식사로 무엇을 먹나요? [정답 : b]
   a. 어떤 어린이들은 아침 식사로 눈송이를 먹어요.
   b. 어떤 어린이들은 아침 식사로 빵을 먹어요.

3. 사진에서, 소녀는 아침 식사로 국수를 먹어요. [정답 : a]
   a. 국수
   b. 빵

Sentence Focus

읽고 알맞은 문장을 고르세요.

1. ☐ 어떤 어린이들은 아침 식사로 과일을 먹어요.
   ■ 어떤 어린이들은 아침 식사로 국수를 먹어요.

2. ■ 모든 어린이는 빵을 먹어요.
   ☐ 모든 어린이는 죽을 먹어요.

3. ☐ 어떤 어린이들은 팬케이크를 먹어요.
   ■ 어떤 어린이들은 콘플레이크를 먹어요.

Word Practice

그림에 알맞은 단어를 찾아 동그라미 하고, 써 보세요.

1. f r i u r a r e i i (e a t) f a t d [eat]
2. t (b r e a d) e e i e r a e a i e a [bread]
3. i r i b e a a t b r (f r u i t) e e [fruit]

Visualization : 주제와 세부사항

주어진 단어를 이용해서 표를 완성하세요.

- (순서대로) Breakfast / noodles
- 주제 – 전 세계의 아침 식사
- 세부사항 – 어떤 어린이들은 빵을 먹어요.
  – 어떤 어린이들은 국수를 먹어요.
  – 어떤 어린이들은 과일을 먹어요.

Talk About It

- 사진에 있는 어린이들은 무엇을 하고 있나요?
- 다른 사람을 돕는 것은 왜 좋은 생각일까요?

Words to Know

듣고 따라 말해 보세요.

- help 돕다
- pick 따다
- giraffe 기린
- corn 옥수수
- plant 심다
- make 만들다
- snore 코를 골다
- popcorn 팝콘

Main Reading

누가 나를 도와줄래?

"내가 옥수수 심는 것 좀 누가 도와줄래?" 기린이 물었어요. "우리가 도와줄게." 고양이와 개가 대답했지요. "내가 옥수수 따는 것 좀 누가 도와줄래?" 기린이 물었어요. "우리가 도와줄게." 고양이와 개가 대답했지요. "내가 팝콘 만드는 것 좀 누가 도와줄래?" 기린이 물었어요. "우리가 도와줄게." 고양이와 개가 대답했지요. "내가 팝콘 먹는 것 좀 누가 도와줄래?" 기린이 물었어요. "우리는 도와줄 수 없어." 고양이와 개가 대답했지요. "아니, 이런!" 기린이 말했어요. "쿨쿨…" 고양이와 개는 코를 골았지요.

Key Expressions

A: 내가 팝콘 만드는 것 좀 누가 도와줄래?

B: 내가 도와줄게.

| 문제 정답 및 해설 |

Comprehension Check

읽고 알맞은 답을 고르세요.

1. 누가 도움을 요청했나요?   [정답 : b]

 a. 고양이와 개

 b. 기린

2. 고양이와 개, 기린은 무엇을 했나요?   [정답 : a]

 a. 옥수수를 땄어요.

 b. 코를 골았어요.

3. 고양이와 개는 기린이 팝콘 만드는 것을 도왔어요.   [정답 : b]

 a. 옥수수

 b. 팝콘

Sentence Focus

읽고 알맞은 문장을 고르세요.

1. ■ 내가 옥수수 따는 것 좀 누가 도와줄래요?

 □ 내가 팝콘 따는 것 좀 누가 도와줄래요?

2. □ 내가 옥수수 먹는 것 좀 누가 도와줄래요?

 ■ 내가 팝콘 먹는 것 좀 누가 도와줄래요?

3. ■ 고양이와 개는 코를 골았지요.

 □ 개와 기린은 코를 골았지요.

Word Practice

그림에 알맞은 단어를 찾아 동그라미 하고, 써 보세요.

1. n p p (c o r n) p i r p e r c o p o   [corn]

2. n l c k o e k r r e c (h e l p) n e   [help]

3. n (p i c k) i i p l h l o k p h k c   [pick]

Visualization : 순서

주어진 단어를 이용해서 표를 완성하세요. 그리고 올바른 순서에 따라 1-4를 써 보세요.

- (순서대로) plant / make
- 1 우리는 옥수수를 심을 거예요.
- 4 우리는 팝콘을 먹을 거예요.
- 3 우리는 팝콘을 만들 거예요.
- 2 우리는 옥수수를 딸 거예요.

Talk About It

· 동물은 언제 잘까요?

· 동물은 얼마나 잘까요?

Words to Know

듣고 따라 말해 보세요.

· animal 동물
· sleep 자다
· day 낮
· night 밤
· a lot 많이
· little 거의 ~않는
· hour 시간
· human 사람

Main Reading

동물의 잠

어떤 동물은 낮에 자요. 어떤 동물은 밤에 자고요. 어떤 동물은 많이 자요. 어떤 동물은 거의 잠을 자지 않아요. 동물들은 잠을 얼마나 잘까요?

동물	일일 평균 총 수면 시간
박쥐	19.9시간
나무늘보	14.4시간
고양이	12.1시간
개	10.6시간
사람	8.6시간
기린	1.9시간

· 이 동물은 하루에 14.4시간을 자요.

· 나는 하루에 8시간을 자요.

· 이 동물은 하루에 12.1시간을 자요.

Key Expressions

A: 고양이들은 잠을 얼마나 자니?

B: 고양이들은 하루에 12.1시간을 자.

| 문제 정답 및 해설 |

Comprehension Check

읽고 알맞은 답을 고르세요.

1. 무엇에 관한 글인가요? [정답 : a]

   a. 동물의 잠에 관한 글이에요.

   b. 동물의 이름에 관한 글이에요.

2. 어떤 동물이 더 많이 자나요? [정답 : a]

   a. 고양이

   b. 기린

3. 사람은 하루에 대략 여덟 시간을 자요. [정답 : b]

   a. 열

   b. 여덟

Sentence Focus

읽고 알맞은 문장을 고르세요.

1. □ 기린은 많이 자요.

   ■ 기린은 거의 잠을 자지 않아요.

2. ■ 박쥐는 낮에 자요.

   □ 박쥐는 밤에 자요.

3. ■ 이 동물은 하루에 14.4시간을 자요.

   □ 이 동물은 하루에 10.6시간을 자요.

Word Practice

그림에 알맞은 단어를 찾아 동그라미 하고, 써 보세요.

1. s d n e y d a a e d a d d a y y e [day]

2. p e a l s l e e p d e a n n y p l [sleep]

3. e p y d a a n i m a l i i l e y s [animal]

Visualization : 주제와 세부사항

주어진 단어를 이용해서 표를 완성하세요.

· (순서대로) Sleep / hours

· 주제 – 동물의 잠

· 세부사항 – 어떤 동물은 낮에 자요. / 어떤 동물은 많이 자요. / 어떤 동물은 하루에 1.9시간을 자요.

Talk About It

- 오늘 날씨는 어떤가요?
- 당신이 가장 좋아하는 날씨는 어떤 날씨인가요?

Words to Know

듣고 따라 말해 보세요.

- wet 젖은, 축축한
- dry 마른
- hot 더운
- cold 추운
- wind 바람
- cloudy 흐린
- rain 비가 오다
- change 변하다

Main Reading

날씨

창밖을 보세요. 땅이 젖어있나요, 아니면 말라있나요? 구름이 있나요? 해가 보이나요? 바람이 부나요? 얼마나 더운가요? 아니면 얼마나 추운가요? 아침에는 날씨가 흐렸어요. 그러다 비가 내렸죠. 이제는 바람도 많이 불어요. 우리가 좋아하든 싫어하든, 날씨는 항상 변해요.

Key Expressions

A: 날씨가 어때?
B: 흐려.

| 문제 정답 및 해설 |

Comprehension Check

읽고 알맞은 답을 고르세요.

1. 무엇에 관한 글인가요?　　　　　　　　[정답 : b]
   a. 창문에 관한 글이에요.
   b. 날씨에 관한 글이에요.

2. 지금 날씨는 어떤가요?　　　　　　　　[정답 : b]
   a. 비가 와요.
   b. 바람이 불어요.

3. 날씨는 항상 변해요.　　　　　　　　　[정답 : a]
   a. 변하다
   b. 비가 오다

Sentence Focus

읽고 알맞은 문장을 고르세요.

1. ■ 오늘은 땅이 젖어있어요.
   □ 오늘은 땅이 말라있어요.

2. □ 아침에는 추웠어요.
   ■ 아침에는 더웠어요.

3. □ 비가 많이 와요.
   ■ 바람이 많이 불어요.

Word Practice

그림에 알맞은 단어를 찾아 동그라미 하고, 써 보세요.

1. r w o c d c (d r y) l d d w d w w r　　　[dry]
2. n y o l d d d r o d y (c o l d) d l　　　[cold]
3. i d i d r c y (w i n d) a d d w n l　　　[wind]

Visualization : 요약

주어진 단어를 이용해서 표를 완성하세요.

- (순서대로) cloudy / changes
- 아침에는 날씨가 흐렸어요.
- 그러다 비가 내렸죠.
- 이제는 바람도 많이 불어요.
  ⇨ 요약 : 날씨는 항상 변해요.

Talk About It

- 당신은 비 오는 날을 좋아하나요?
- 당신은 비 오는 날에 무엇을 하고 싶은가요?

Words to Know

듣고 따라 말해 보세요.

- tangram 칠교놀이
- triangle 삼각형
- rectangle 직사각형
- thing 물건
- puzzle 퍼즐
- square 사각형
- people 사람들
- quickly 빨리

Main Reading

칠교놀이를 해요

밖에는 비가 와요. 칠교놀이를 하기에 딱 좋은 날이지요. 칠교는 중국식 퍼즐이에요. 큰 정사각형이나 직사각형, 삼각형을 만들 수 있어요. 동물 모양도 만들 수 있어요. 사람 모양도 만들 수 있지요. 물건 모양도 만들 수 있어요. 당신도 칠교놀이를 해보고 싶나요? 당신이 얼마나 빨리 각각의 퍼즐을 만들 수 있는지 보세요. 재밌게 놀아요!

Key Expressions

A: 너는 무엇을 만들 수 있니?
B: 나는 고양이 모양을 만들 수 있어.

| 문제 정답 및 해설 |

Comprehension Check

읽고 알맞은 답을 고르세요.

1. 무엇에 관한 글인가요? [정답 : a]
   a. 칠교놀이가 무엇인지에 관한 글이에요.
   b. 완벽한 날에 관한 글이에요.

2. 칠교놀이로 무엇을 할 수 있나요? [정답 : b]
   a. 사람들을 만날 수 있어요.
   b. 동물 모양을 만들 수 있어요.

3. 사진에서, 고양이 모양을 만들기 위해 칠교 조각 일곱개가 사용되었어요. [정답 : a]
   a. 일곱
   b. 여덟

Sentence Focus

읽고 알맞은 문장을 고르세요.

1. ☐ 밖에서 놀기에 딱 좋은 날이에요.
   ■ 퍼즐놀이를 하기에 딱 좋은 날이에요.

2. ■ 동물 모양을 만들 수 있어요.
   ☐ 사람 모양을 만들 수 있어요.

3. ■ 큰 정사각형을 만들 수 있어요.
   ☐ 큰 삼각형을 만들 수 있어요.

Word Practice

그림에 알맞은 단어를 찾아 동그라미 하고, 써 보세요.

1. p l e e u g p i z p p e t h i n g [thing]
2. t p e e i p e o p l e e n p n n l [people]
3. e z p t i e p e p u z z l e p t p [puzzle]

Visualization : 주제와 세부사항

주어진 단어를 이용해서 표를 완성하세요.

- (순서대로) Chinese / things / quickly
- 주제 – 칠교놀이
- 세부사항 – 중국식 퍼즐이에요.
  - 동물, 사람, 물건 모양을 만들 수 있어요.
  - 각각의 퍼즐을 빨리 만드는 것이 재미있어요.

Talk About It

- 사람을 돕는 개를 본 적이 있나요?
- 개는 어떻게 사람을 도울까요?

Words to Know

듣고 따라 말해 보세요.

- bark 짖다
- search 찾아보다
- snow 눈
- leap 뛰다
- hole 구멍
- dig 파다
- trapped 갇힌
- wag 흔들다

Main Reading

정말 멋진 팀이에요!

"멍멍!" 케빈이 구멍을 향해 짖어요. 나는 케빈에게 달려가지요. 그리고 케빈에게 "찾아봐!"라고 명령해요. 케빈은 재빨리 구멍을 더 크게 파요. 그리고 나는 눈 속에 갇힌 사람을 끌어내지요. "잘했어, 케빈. 잘했어!" 나는 케빈을 쓰다듬어요. 케빈은 뛰어오르며 꼬리를 흔들지요. 케빈과 나, 우리는 정말 멋진 팀이에요!

Key Expressions

A: 개가 사람을 어떻게 도울까?
B: 어떤 개들은 사람을 구조해.

| 문제 정답 및 해설 |

Comprehension Check

읽고 알맞은 답을 고르세요.

1. 케빈은 왜 짖나요? [정답 : b]
   a. 케빈이 눈 속에 갇혔기 때문이에요.
   b. 케빈이 눈 속에 갇힌 남자를 찾았기 때문이에요.

2. 케빈은 무엇을 하나요? [정답 : a]
   a. 구멍을 더 크게 파요.
   b. 남자를 끌어내요.

3. 케빈은 구조견이에요. [정답 : b]
   a. 소년
   b. 개

Sentence Focus

읽고 알맞은 문장을 고르세요.

1. ■ 케빈이 구멍을 향해 짖어요.
   □ 케빈이 구멍을 더 크게 파요.

2. □ 나는 케빈에게 명령해요.
   ■ 나는 눈 속에 갇힌 남자를 끌어내요.

3. ■ 케빈이 길에서 뛰어올라요.
   □ 케빈이 꼬리를 흔들어요.

Word Practice

그림에 알맞은 단어를 찾아 동그라미 하고, 써 보세요.

1. d e e o p l r r c t a h o l e a e [hole]
2. c h l h t o p o s e a r c h l o r [search]
3. e o a c d p e a t r a p p e d o d [trapped]

Visualization : 이야기의 구성요소

주어진 단어를 이용해서 표를 완성하세요.

- (순서대로) order / snow

누가?	무엇을?	왜?
· 케빈과 나	1. 케빈이 구멍을 향해 짖어요. 2. 케빈에게 "찾아봐!"라고 명령해요. 3. 케빈은 재빨리 구멍을 더 크게 파요.	· 케빈과 나는 눈 속에 갇힌 남자를 구해야 해요.

Talk About It

- 사진에서 무엇이 보이나요?
- 쥐는 무엇을 할까요?

Words to Know

듣고 따라 말해 보세요.

- hide 숨다
- caterpillar 애벌레
- jaguar 재규어
- pattern 무늬
- hard 어려운
- branch 나뭇가지
- nest 둥지
- wild 야생

Main Reading

위장

야생에서 동물들은 어떻게 숨을까요? 이 애벌레는 나뭇가지 위에 있으면 잘 보이지 않아요. 이 재규어는 나무에 있으면 찾기 힘들지요. 이 물고기는 모래 속에 있으면 잘 보이지 않아요. 이 알들은 둥지 안에 있으면 찾기 힘들지요. 이 새들은 풀 속에 있으면 잘 보이지 않아요. 이 뱀도 나무에 있으면 잘 보이지 않아요. 동물들은 야생에서 숨기 위해 색깔이나 무늬를 이용해요.

Key Expressions

A: 동물들은 어떻게 숨을까?
B: 그들은 숨기 위해 색깔을 이용해.

| 문제 정답 및 해설 |

Comprehension Check

읽고 알맞은 답을 고르세요.

1. 무엇에 관한 글인가요? [정답 : a]
   a. 동물들이 어떻게 숨는지에 관한 글이에요.
   b. 동물들이 어떻게 보는지에 관한 글이에요.

2. 재규어는 왜 나무에서 잘 안 보이나요? [정답 : a]
   a. 재규어는 숨기 위해 패턴을 이용하기 때문이에요.
   b. 재규어는 숨기 위해 눈을 이용하기 때문이에요.

3. 동물들은 야생에서 숨기 위해 색깔이나 무늬를 이용해요.
   a. 놀다 [정답 : b]
   b. 숨다

Sentence Focus

읽고 알맞은 문장을 고르세요.

1. ■ 이 물고기는 모래 속에 있으면 잘 보이지 않아요.
   □ 이 알은 모래 속에 있으면 잘 보이지 않아요.

2. ■ 이 새는 나무에 있으면 잘 보이지 않아요.
   □ 이 새는 풀 속에 있으면 잘 보이지 않아요.

3. ■ 이 뱀은 야생에서 숨기 위해 색깔을 이용해요.
   □ 이 뱀은 야생에서 숨기 위해 무늬를 이용해요.

Word Practice

그림에 알맞은 단어를 찾아 동그라미 하고, 써 보세요.

1. b r a n c h r n n r r h r e c h a d [branch]
2. d h n n n b a i d d b h h i d e h [hide]
3. c b i i e e c w i l d e e a w d i [wild]

Visualization : 주제와 세부사항

주어진 단어를 이용해서 표를 완성하세요.

- (순서대로) hide / patterns
- 주제 – 동물들은 야생에서 다른 동물을 피해 숨어요.
- 세부사항 – 어떤 동물들은 숨기 위해 색깔을 이용해요.
  – 어떤 동물들은 숨기 위해 무늬를 이용해요.

Talk About It

- 당신은 엽서를 받거나 보낸 적이 있나요?
- 사람들은 언제 엽서를 보낼까요?

Words to Know

듣고 따라 말해 보세요.

- weather 날씨
- winter 겨울
- dogsled racing 개썰매 경주
- ice hotel 얼음 호텔
- Canada 캐나다
- carnival 축제
- snow tubing 튜브 눈썰매
- visit 방문하다

Main Reading

겨울 축제

할머니께,

저는 캐나다 퀘벡에서 편지를 쓰고 있어요. 날씨는 춥고 눈이 와요. 저는 퀘벡 겨울 축제에 방문했어요. 저는 개썰매 경주를 즐겼어요. 저는 튜브를 타고 눈썰매를 즐겼어요. 저는 얼음 호텔에 머무는 것을 즐겼어요. 여기 퀘벡에 있는 것이 좋아요. 할머니께서도 여기에 방문하셔야 해요! 다음에는 함께 여기에 올 수 있으면 좋겠어요. 사랑을 담아서, 사라 드림

Key Expressions

A: 퀘벡에서 너는 무엇을 했니?
B: 개썰매 경주를 즐겼어.

| 문제 정답 및 해설 |

Comprehension Check

읽고 알맞은 답을 고르세요.

1. 사라는 어디에 방문했나요? [정답 : a]
   a. 그녀는 퀘벡 겨울 축제에 방문했어요.
   b. 그녀는 퀘벡에 있는 할머니 댁에 방문했어요.

2. 사라는 겨울 축제에서 무엇을 즐겼나요? [정답 : a]
   a. 그녀는 튜브 눈썰매를 즐겼어요.
   b. 그녀는 스케이트를 즐겼어요.

3. 사라는 그녀의 할머니에게 엽서를 쓰고 있어요. [정답 : b]
   a. 친구
   b. 할머니

Sentence Focus

읽고 알맞은 문장을 고르세요.

1. ■ 나는 캐나다에 방문했어.
   □ 나는 한국에 방문했어.

2. □ 나는 개썰매 경주를 즐겼어.
   ■ 나는 튜브를 타고 눈썰매를 즐겼어.

3. ■ 나는 얼음 호텔에 머물렀어.
   □ 나는 텐트에 머물렀어.

Word Practice

그림에 알맞은 단어를 찾아 동그라미 하고, 써 보세요.

1. n w (w i n t e r) i a i i c l i i r [winter]
2. a d (c a r n i v a l) c c s i n r c [carnival]
3. r e n i i s l a n r n (v i s i t) e [visit]

Visualization : 주제와 세부사항

주어진 단어를 이용해서 표를 완성하세요.

- (순서대로) Winter / ice hotel
- 주제 – 퀘벡 겨울 축제
- 세부사항 – 나는 개썰매 경주를 즐겼어요.
  – 나는 튜브를 타고 눈썰매를 즐겼어요.
  – 나는 얼음 호텔에 머무는 것을 즐겼어요.

Talk About It

- 당신은 오늘 점심으로 무엇을 먹고 싶나요?
- 전 세계에 있는 어린이들은 무엇을 먹을까요?

Words to Know

듣고 따라 말해 보세요.

- local 현지의
- crab 게
- grilled 구운
- bottled water 병에 든 생수
- add 추가하다
- green salad 야채 샐러드
- drink 음료
- take-out 포장해 가는 음식

Main Reading

점심은 무엇인가요?

알래스카 피시 하우스 −케치캔 점−

〈생선〉

	두 조각	세 조각
대구	10달러	12달러
지역 특산 연어	11달러	13달러
지역 특산 넙치	16달러	18달러

〈게〉

거미게 ½파운드	14달러	거미게 1파운드	27달러
킹크랩 ½파운드	22달러	킹크랩 1파운드	43달러

〈샐러드〉

야채 샐러드	5달러		
구운 연어 추가	6달러	구운 넙치 추가	7달러

〈음료〉

탄산음료	(소) 1달러	(대) 2달러	
오렌지 주스	3달러	병에 든 생수	2달러

특별 할인 시간!
월−금 오후 3시에서 6시까지
"포장도 가능합니다."

Key Expressions

A: 점심으로 무엇을 드실 건가요?
B: 지역 특산 연어로 주세요.

| 문제 정답 및 해설 |

Comprehension Check

읽고 알맞은 답을 고르세요.

1. 이 글은 무엇인가요? [정답 : b]
   a. 쿠폰이에요.　　b. 메뉴예요.

2. 대구는 두 조각에 얼마인가요? [정답 : a]
   a. 10달러　　b. 11달러

3. 야채 샐러드를 먹으려면 5달러가 필요해요.
   a. 5달러　　b. 9달러 [정답 : a]

Sentence Focus

읽고 알맞은 문장을 고르세요.

1. ■ 지역 특산 넙치를 먹고 싶어요.
   □ 킹크랩을 먹고 싶어요.

2. □ 25달러가 있으니 거미게 1파운드를 먹을 수 있어요.
   ■ 25달러가 있으니 킹크랩 1/2파운드를 먹을 수 있어요.

3. □ 작은 탄산음료 마시는 데 2달러가 필요해요.
   ■ 큰 탄산음료 마시는 데 2달러가 필요해요.

Word Practice

그림에 알맞은 단어를 찾아 동그라미 하고, 써 보세요.

1. g d e r b r a l (a d d) d a d g a a [add]
2. g d r g (c r a b) l c b g a d a g c [crab]
3. (g r i l l e d) i c e l g l r a d i [grilled]

Visualization : 분류

주어진 단어를 이용해서 표를 완성하세요.

- (순서대로) FIsh / Drinks

생선과 게	샐러드	음료
·대구 ·연어	·야채 샐러드	·작은 탄산음료
·넙치 ·거미게	·구운 연어 샐러드	·큰 탄산음료
·킹크랩	·구운 넙치 샐러드	·오렌지 주스
		·병에 든 생수

Talk About It

- 사과 한 개를 물에 넣으면 어떤 일이 일어날까요?
- 사과는 물 위에 뜰까요, 물에 가라앉을까요?

Words to Know

듣고 따라 말해 보세요.

- splash 첨벙거리다
- bubble 거품
- sink 가라앉다
- tub 욕조
- bath 욕조, 목욕
- wonder 궁금해하다
- float 뜨다
- soap 비누

Main Reading

물에 가라앉을까요? 아니면 물 위에 뜰까요?

앤디는 욕조에서 물장구치는 것을 좋아해요. 이것은 작은 고무 오리 장난감이에요. 앤디와 목욕 시간을 함께 하는 친구죠. 고무 오리는 꽥꽥 소리를 낼 수 있어요. 거품을 만들 수도 있어요. 앤디는 궁금해요. '이 고무 오리가 물에 가라앉을까? 아니면 물 위에 뜰까?' 앤디는 작은 고무 오리 장난감을 욕조 속으로 떨어뜨려요. 고무 오리가 물 위에 떠요! 앤디는 비누와 칫솔, 빗, 스펀지를 찾아내요. 한번에 하나씩, 앤디는 이 물건들을 욕조에 넣어요. 과연 이 물건들은 물에 가라앉을까요? 아니면 물 위에 뜰까요?

Key Expressions

A: 비누는 물에 가라앉을까? 아니면 물 위에 뜰까?
B: 물에 가라앉을 거야.

| 문제 정답 및 해설 |

Comprehension Check

읽고 알맞은 답을 고르세요.

1. 앤디는 어디에 있나요?　　　　　　　　[정답 : b]
   a. 침실에 있어요.
   b. 욕실에 있어요.

2. 앤디는 무엇을 하나요?　　　　　　　　[정답 : b]
   a. 거품을 만들어요.
   b. 욕조에서 물장구를 쳐요.

3. 작은 고무 오리 장난감은 물 위에 떠요.　[정답 : a]
   a. 떠요
   b. 가라앉아요

Sentence Focus

읽고 알맞은 문장을 고르세요.

1. ☐ 고무 오리는 거품을 만들 수 있어요.
   ■ 고무 오리는 꽥꽥 소리를 낼 수 있어요.

2. ☐ 그는 욕조에 칫솔을 떨어뜨려요.
   ■ 그는 욕조에 스펀지를 떨어뜨려요.

3. ☐ 그는 거품 만들기를 좋아해요.
   ■ 그는 욕조에서 물장구치는 것을 좋아해요.

Word Practice

그림에 알맞은 단어를 찾아 동그라미 하고, 써 보세요.

1. w w e k b h h b o a b k b a t h w 　　[bath]
2. e b b r d t w o n d e r t b w d e 　　[wonder]
3. k n d n i s e s k a d e o s i n k 　　[sink]

Visualization : 분류

주어진 단어를 이용해서 표를 완성하세요.

- (왼쪽부터) sponge / Sink

뜨다	가라앉다
작은 고무 오리 장난감	빗
스펀지	비누
칫솔	

Talk About It

• 모양을 바꿀 수 있는 것은 무엇인가요?

• 크기를 바꿀 수 있는 것은 무엇인가요?

Words to Know

듣고 따라 말해 보세요.

- look 보다
- desk 책상
- solid 고체
- liquid 액체
- gas 기체
- shape 모양
- size 크기
- matter 물질

Main Reading

물질을 발견해요

주위를 둘러보세요. 여러분이 보고 있는 것의 대부분이 바로 물질이에요. 책상은 물질이에요. 책상은 고체이지요. 고체는 모양이 있어요. 우유도 물질이에요. 우유는 액체이지요. 액체는 모양을 바꿀 수 있어요. 공 속의 공기도 물질이에요. 공 안의 공기는 기체이지요. 기체는 모양과 크기를 바꿀 수 있어요. 고체, 액체, 기체는 모두 물질이에요. 고체, 액체, 기체는 언제나 여러분 주위에 있어요.

Key Expressions

A: 무엇이 모양을 바꿀 수 있지?

B: 액체와 기체는 모양을 바꿀 수 있어.

| 문제 정답 및 해설 |

Comprehension Check

읽고 알맞은 답을 고르세요.

1. 무엇에 관한 글인가요?   [정답 : a]

  a. 물질에 관한 글이에요.

  b. 크기에 관한 글이에요.

2. 어디에서 물질을 볼 수 있나요?   [정답 : a]

  a. 어디서든 볼 수 있어요.

  b. 공 안에서만 볼 수 있어요.

3. 기체는 모양과 크기를 바꿀 수 있어요.   [정답 : a]

  a. 기체

  b. 고체

Sentence Focus

읽고 알맞은 문장을 고르세요.

1. ■ 책상은 고체예요.

  □ 책상은 기체예요.

2. □ 공 안의 공기는 액체예요.

  ■ 공 안의 공기는 기체예요.

3. ■ 액체는 모양을 바꿀 수 있어요.

  □ 고체는 모양을 바꿀 수 있어요.

Word Practice

그림에 알맞은 단어를 찾아 동그라미 하고, 써 보세요.

1. l a l g s (l o o k) d s a l a s o k   [look]

2. d l (s o l i d) o i s s o o g d i s   [solid]

3. s o i s k s k (g a s) o o i l g o s   [gas]

Visualization : 분류

주어진 단어를 이용해서 표를 완성하세요.

· (순서대로) Solid / milk / size

물질		
고체	액체	기체
– 책상	– 우유	– 공 안의 공기
– 모양이 있어요.	– 모양을 바꿀 수 있어요.	– 모양과 크기를 바꿀 수 있어요.

Talk About It

- 사진 속에 있는 어린이들은 무엇을 하고 있나요?
- 사진 속의 물을 마시는 것이 안전하다고 생각하나요?

Words to Know

듣고 따라 말해 보세요.

- dirty 더러운
- clean 깨끗한
- skin 피부
- stomach 배
- head 머리
- hurt 아프게 하다
- wake 일어나다
- get 얻다

Main Reading

아요 이야기

아요는 잠비아에서 살아요. 아요는 언니 아마라와 함께 살지요. 잠비아의 물은 매우 더러워요. 그 물은 아요의 피부를 아프게 해요. 아요의 배도 아프게 하고요. 아요의 머리도 아프게 해요. 매일 아침 아마라는 해가 뜨기 전에 일어나요. 아마라는 아요를 위한 물을 길어 오려고 2마일을 걸어요. 아마라는 아요를 위한 물을 길어 오려고 하루에 세 번 걷지요. 아요는 아마라에게 미안해요. 아요는 잠비아에서 깨끗한 물을 마실 수 있기를 바라요.

Key Expressions

A: 더러운 물을 마시면 무슨 일이 일어날까?
B: 그 물이 내 피부를 아프게 할 거야.

| 문제 정답 및 해설 |

Comprehension Check

읽고 알맞은 답을 고르세요.

1. 누구에 관한 이야기인가요?　　　　　　　　[정답 : b]
   a. 잠비아에 관한 이야기예요.
   b. 아요에 관한 이야기예요.

2. 잠비아에서는 무엇이 문제인가요?　　　　　[정답 : b]
   a. 공기가 매우 더러워요.
   b. 물이 매우 더러워요.

3. 아요는 잠비아의 물이 깨끗하길 바라요.　　[정답 : a]
   a. 깨끗한
   b. 더러운

Sentence Focus

읽고 알맞은 문장을 고르세요.

1. ■ 그녀는 언니와 함께 살아요.
   □ 그녀는 엄마와 함께 살아요.

2. □ 그녀는 아요보다 먼저 일어나요.
   ■ 그녀는 해가 뜨기 전에 일어나요.

3. ■ 그녀는 물을 길어 오려고 2마일을 걸어요.
   □ 그녀는 언니를 보려고 2마일을 걸어요.

Word Practice

그림에 알맞은 단어를 찾아 동그라미 하고, 써 보세요.

1. s i h t (s k i n) h t m a u s c o r　　　　[skin]
2. h t i h (s t o m a c h) c k r s i u　　　　[stomach]
3. h u o s h n c k m h n a o (h u r t)　　　[hurt]

Visualization : 원인과 결과

주어진 단어를 이용해서 표를 완성하세요.

- (순서대로) dirty / water

왜인가요?	무슨 일이 일어났나요?
· 잠비아의 물은 매우 더러워요.	⇨ 아요는 아파요.
· 아요는 아파요.	⇨ 아마라는 아요를 위한 물을 길어 오려고 2마일을 걸어요.

Talk About It

- 깨끗한 물을 마시는 것은 왜 중요할까요?
- 어떻게 더러운 물을 깨끗하게 만들 수 있을까요?

Words to Know

듣고 따라 말해 보세요.

- drink 마시다
- charcoal 숯
- rock 돌
- top 위
- cloth 천
- sand 모래
- cap 뚜껑
- slowly 천천히

Main Reading

깨끗한 물을 만드는 방법

여러분은 깨끗한 물을 마셔야 해요. 이것이 바로 깨끗한 물을 만들 수 있는 방법이에요.

준비물 : 더러운 물, 물병, 천 두 조각, 숯, 모래, 작은 돌 몇 개

1. 물병 뚜껑에 구멍 다섯 개를 뚫어 주세요.
2. 천 조각 하나를 물병 안에 넣어 주세요.
3. 약간의 모래와 작은 돌들을 그 위에 넣어 주세요.
4. 숯을 위에 넣어 주세요.
5. 나머지 천 한 조각을 그 위에 넣어 주세요.
6. 그 위에 더러운 물을 천천히 부어 주세요.
7. 조금만 기다리면, 깨끗한 물을 얻게 될 거예요.

Key Expressions

A: 어떻게 깨끗한 물을 만들 수 있을까?
B: 우선 뚜껑에 구멍 다섯 개를 뚫어.

| 문제 정답 및 해설 |

Comprehension Check

읽고 알맞은 답을 고르세요.

1. 무엇에 관한 글인가요?　　　　　　　　　　　　　[정답 : b]
   a. 깨끗한 물을 마시는 방법에 관한 글이에요.
   b. 깨끗한 물을 만드는 방법에 관한 글이에요.

2. 깨끗한 물을 만드는 데 필요하지 않은 것은 무엇인가요?
   a. 깨끗한 물　　　　　　　　　　　　　　　　　[정답 : a]
   b. 더러운 물

3. 물병 뚜껑에 구멍을 뚫어야 해요.　　　　　　　　[정답 : a]
   a. 뚜껑
   b. 천

Sentence Focus

읽고 알맞은 문장을 고르세요.

1. ▢ 천 조각 하나를 맨 위에 넣어 주세요.
   ■ 작은 돌 몇 개를 맨 위에 넣어 주세요.

2. ■ 숯을 위에 넣어 주세요.
   ▢ 약간의 모래를 위에 넣어 주세요.

3. ▢ 더러운 물을 만들어 주세요.
   ■ 더러운 물을 부어 주세요.

Word Practice

그림에 알맞은 단어를 찾아 동그라미 하고, 써 보세요.

1. o k o k t r o k (d r i n k) t t k t　　　　[drink]
2. (t o p) p d o k r r c c o n p c k o　　　　[top]
3. i k o o r c o d i o k (r o c k) n n　　　　[rock]

Visualization : 순서

주어진 단어를 이용해서 표를 완성하세요. 그리고 올바른 순서에 따라 1-4를 써 보세요.

- (순서대로) charcoal / sand
- 3 숯을 맨 위에 넣어 주세요.
  4 그 위에 더러운 물을 천천히 부어 주세요.
  1 천 조각 하나를 물병 안에 넣어 주세요.
  2 약간의 모래와 작은 돌들을 그 위에 넣어 주세요.

미국교과서 READING Level 2 권별 교과 목록

1권 2.1

1. Social Studies
2. Language Arts
3. Health & Wellness
4. Language Arts
5. Health & Wellness
6. Social Studies
7. Social Studies
8. Health & Wellness
9. Social Studies
10. Science
11. Science
12. Math
13. Social Studies
14. Science
15. Social Studies
16. Math
17. Science
18. Science
19. Ethics
20. Science

2권 2.2

1. Health & Wellness
2. Science
3. Language Arts
4. Social Studies
5. Language Arts
6. Health & Wellness
7. Language Arts
8. Social Studies
9. Language Arts
10. Science
11. Language Arts
12. Language Arts
13. Ethics
14. Ethics
15. Language Arts
16. Science
17. Language Arts
18. Art & Crafts
19. Language Arts
20. Ethics

3권 2.3

1. Social Studies
2. Art & Crafts
3. Health & Wellness
4. Social Studies
5. Language Arts
6. Social Studies
7. Ethics
8. Social Studies
9. Language Arts
10. Science
11. Language Arts
12. Science
13. Social Studies
14. Science
15. Science
16. Science
17. Social Studies
18. Social Studies
19. Language Arts
20. Science

길벗스쿨 공식 카페, <기적의 공부방>에서 함께 공부해요!

기적의 학습단

홈스쿨링 응원 프로젝트! 학습단에 참여하여 공부 습관도 기르고 칭찬 선물도 받으세요!

도서 서평단

길벗스쿨의 책을 가장 먼저 체험하고, 기획에도 직접 참여해 보세요.

알찬 학습 팁

엄마표 학습 노하우를 나누며 우리 아이 맞춤 학습법을 함께 찾아요.

<기적의 공부방> https://cafe.naver.com/gilbutschool